The Title of the Letter

SUNY Series in Contemporary Continental Philosophy

Dennis J. Schmidt, editor

THE TITLE OF THE LETTER
A Reading of Lacan

Jean-Luc Nancy and Philippe Lacoue-Labarthe

Translated by
François Raffoul and
David Pettigrew

State University of New York Press

Le titre de la lettre
was originally published in French © 1973 ÉDITIONS GALILÉE

Published by
State University of New York Press, Albany

© 1992   State University of New York

Printed in the United States of America

For information, address State University of New York
Press, State University Plaza, Albany, N.Y. 12246

Production by Dana Foote
Marketing by Theresa A. Swierzowski

Library of Congress Cataloging-in-Publication Data

Lacoue-Labarthe, Philippe.
    [Titre de la lettre. English]
    The title of the letter : a reading of Lacan / Jean-Luc Nancy and
Philippe Lacoue-Labarthe ; translated by François Raffoul and
David Pettigrew.
       p. cm. — (SUNY series in contemporary continental
philosophy)
    Translation of: Le titre de la lettre.
    Includes bibliographical references and index.
    ISBN 0–7914–0961–9 (alk. paper) — ISBN 0–7914–0962–7 (pbk. :
alk. paper)
    1. Lacan, Jacques, 1901–   I. Nancy, Jean-Luc. II. Title.
III. Series.
BF109.L28A313   1992
150. 19'5'092—dc20
                                        91–15114
                                          CIP

10 9 8 7 6 5 4 3

Contents

Translators' Preface

In 1973, Jacques Lacan presented a seminar, later published in *Encore,* entitled *God and the Jouissance of the Woman.*[1] Lacan began the seminar by advising his audience to read a book, which had been published only recently, entitled: *The Title of the Letter: A Reading of Lacan,* by Philippe Lacoue-Labarthe and Jean-Luc Nancy.[2] Despite the fact that the text presented itself explicitly as a deconstruction of his work, and did indeed deconstruct it rigorously, Lacan praised the text highly, although he took issue with its conclusion. "It is," he said at the outset, "with the greatest satisfaction that I have read it. I could not encourage its distribution enough" (*XX.,* 62). Lacan asserted, moreover, that:

> I can say, in a way, if it is a question of reading, that I have never been read so well—with so much love....
>
> We shall say, then, that this is a model of good reading, so much so that I am able to say that I regret never having obtained anything that comes close to it from my followers.... (*XX.,* 62)

Lacan continued by saying that "the work develops in a way such that I am compelled to acknowledge its remarkably explanatory value." He concluded his remarks by strongly recommending the text to his audience, although he expressed reservations with respect to the "last twenty or thirty pages," which focus on certain limits of the Lacanian "subversion" (*XX.,* 63).

Not surprisingly, Lacan resisted the type of interpretation that he was subjected to, particularly in that second half of the book, where Lacoue-Labarthe and Nancy attempt to show

how he paradoxically reinscribes (indeed, sublates) a number of philosophical motifs that he had sought to subvert. (One example, as we will see, is the motif of subjectivity: if indeed the Lacanian subject is eclipsed by the order of the signifier, the authors claim that it is nevertheless maintained, through its punctuality and a decisive relation to science as a calculus, as a Cartesian subject through and through.) Starting from a highly rigorous commentary of the first part of "The Agency of the Letter" ("The Meaning of the Letter"), where the authors demonstrate how Lacan's *diversion* of linguistics amounts to a challenging of the traditional theoretical order, they proceed to reveal, in the last two parts of the *Agency* ("The Letter in the Unconscious" and "The Letter, Being, and the Other") a paradoxical reconstruction of that very theoretical order. They suggest that it is as if there were, in the logic of the signifier established by Lacan, a "systematic force at work that does not cease to reconstruct or recenter what Lacan's critique of 'monocentrism' aims at destroying or exceeding" (*TL.,* 113). In that respect Lacoue-Labarthe and Nancy's work exceeds being merely a commentary (*TL.,* 87), but rather amounts to a *strategy of reading* which they place under the authority of deconstruction; in particular, the kind of deconstruction practiced by Jacques Derrida (*TL.,* 92).

Indeed, this text, published first in 1973, was presented as part of a seminar led by Jacques Derrida at the École Normale Supérieure in May 1972. In a footnote in *Le Facteur de la Vérité,* Derrida wrote, "for a rigorous reading of Lacan [I refer] to the fundamental and indispensable book by Jean-Luc Nancy and Philippe Lacoue-Labarthe, *The Title of the Letter.*"[3]

In the nineteen years since its publication, *The Title of the Letter* has been distinguished as the principle reference for a philosophical approach to Lacan's work, an approach which is authorized, so to speak, by Lacoue-Labarthe and Nancy's claim that, in a sense, Lacan's text "is proposed straightaway and openly as a *philosophical* text."[4] The book has been translated into Spanish, Italian, and Portugese, and has had three editions in French. One may wonder, then, why the text has not found its way into English until now. A number of Lacoue-Labarthe and Nancy's other works, whether written together or separately, have already appeared in English.[5] Now, however, with the support of William Eastman, director of SUNY Press, the text will be available to the English language audience and will enrich philosophical and literary discourse with respect to Lacan's work.

As the authors state, *The Title of the Letter: A Reading of Lacan* is a close reading of *one* of Jacques Lacan's essays, "The Agency of the Letter in the Unconscious or Reason since Freud." The authors articulate three moments in Lacan's text. In the first moment, that of the commentary, they follow Lacan's *diversion* of Saussurean linguistics—a diversion which is to be understood as a subversion, indeed, as a destruction of the linguistic theory of the sign. In the second moment, they show how Lacan's science of the letter, which was established on the basis of the diversion of linguistics, articulates itself with psychoanalysis through "a certain relation *between the letter and truth,* insofar as *desire* is implicated therein" (*TL.,* 82). What is at issue, then, is reading psychoanalysis through linguistics (as exemplified in the *literal* transcriptions or transpositions of the major elements of Freud's conceptual apparatus) and linguistics through psychoanalysis (as exemplified in the interpretation of the bar separating the signifier and the signified as the symbolic bar of repression). Ultimately proving undecidable, the relationship between the two disciplines, however, calls for yet another articulation. In the third moment, the authors demonstrate that the science of the letter articulates itself onto another register, that of the philosophical. At this stage, they abandon their commentary per se and reveal a system in Lacan's text which is determined by, and reinscribes, a number of classical philosophical presuppositions: the certainty of subjectivity, systematicity, and the positing of a ground.

A look at the title of the text brings us right into the first moment of Lacoue-Labarthe and Nancy's work, concerning Lacan's diversion of linguistics. As they indicate, the title of the text, *The Title of the Letter,* should be understood in two ways: not only as one speaks of the title of a book but also in the sense of a title that establishes a right of property, a status or position, or validates a claim (*TL.,* 2). The claim or right in question is that of the *Letter* of Lacan's "The Agency of the Letter in the Unconscious or Reason since Freud," a title or a right which they propose to "produce, decipher, and authenticate" (*TL.,* 2).

The first moment of their text follows Lacan's diversion and radicalization of Saussurean linguistics. Lacan's point of departure, as we know, is the rejection of any mythical notion of the unconscious as the seat of instincts, a rejection of any sort of depth psychology. The subject—that is, the subject revealed by psychoanalysis—is to be understood simply as an effect of the signifier, a subject of the letter. Or, should we say, a subject *subjected* to the letter. Indeed, Lacoue-Labarthe and Nancy significantly speak of a "literalization of the subject" (*TL.,* 27), to the extent that the letter is defined as the structure of language insofar as the subject is implicated therein. The subject, if only mediated by its proper name, comes to itself in and through language. This explains Lacan's recourse to linguistics, and why the articulation of a theory of the subject, given that point of departure, must then "go through" a theory of language. As they comment, "one must thus adjust a theory of the subject...to this 'emergence' of linguistics" (*TL.,* 32). This adjustment is not, however, a simple submission to linguistics, specifically to Saussurean linguistics. Rather, the issue for Lacan is to "locate" or to "seek" the science of the letter *in* linguistics. It is not surprising, then, if in fact Lacan subjects Saussurean linguistics and its theory of the sign to what Lacoue-Labarthe and Nancy, following Lacan himself, identify as a *diversion.* Such a diversion, indeed, focuses on the sign, whose theory is considered as nothing less than what "constitutes linguistics as a science."[6] The *coup de force* consists in a certain formalization of the Saussurean sign, rendered as this algorithm:

$$\frac{S}{s}$$

This algorithm is to be understood, they advise us, in the strict sense of a procedure of algebraic calculus, of differential notation, "a pure calculus conforming to the isolated and localized structure of the signifier." While it has often been said that Lacan's diversion or "appropriation" (to use a term that will prove inappropriate) of linguistics and its theory of the sign consists in the autonomization of the signifier—certainly a correct assessment—Lacoue-Labarthe and Nancy claim that this autonomy is secondary with respect to the main issue in Lacan's diversion: the emphasis placed on the bar separating the signifier from the signified. Moreover, the autonomy of the signifier rests on the fact that the bar *resists* access of the signifier to the signified. This resistance is conceived in such a way that "whereas for Saussure, what is essential is the *relation* (the reciprocity, or the association), Lacan introduces a resistance such that the crossing of the bar, the relation of the signifier to the signified, in short, the production of signification itself, will never be self-evident" (*TL.,* 36). For Saussure, the line between the signifier and signified suggests two different registers. The value of each signifier is determined by its differential negativity with respect to the totality of the other signifiers, yet for Saussure, each *signifier* ultimately refers to its particular *signified* in an arbitrary coupling according to linguistic convention. However, for Lacan the line between the two registers is a *bar* indicating that the signifier has *no* access to its signified. The signifier is left to slide in a field of signifiers, seeking its signified, yet encountering nothing but other signifiers. And if each signifier refers only to another signifier which, in turn, refers to yet another signifier, then one is faced with nothing less than a systemic indeterminacy. With the subversion of the sign, the signifier becomes an autonomous function—a function that Lacan calls, as we just saw, "*algorithmic.*"

In this destruction of the parallelism between the orders of signifier and signified, and the dismantling of the structural unity of the sign, Saussurean linguistics is itself detroyed. Or rather, Saussurean linguistics as it is constituted by a theory of the sign. Language is *not* to be thought on the basis of the sign. The algorithm, *unlike* the sign, does not signify, if what is implied by this term is a representation of a signified; the algorithm, *unlike* the sign, does not signify for *someone*.[7] Now, as we know, in the science of the letter, the signifier does not represent something (a signified) for someone, but rather *represents the subject for another signifier*. This institutes the science of the letter as a *"linguistics without a theory of the sign"* (*TL.,* 36), or as Lacan mischieveously baptized it in *Encore:* a *linguisterie,* which one could render as *"linguis-trickery"* (*XX.,* 20). The diversion of the sign amounts to displacing both the referentiality to which the sign is traditionally submitted and the subjectivity for which it is traditionally supposed to function. The signifier functions as an algorithm, that is, in a chain of differential marks which signify nothing but their differential and reciprocal positions. Consequently, the process of signification, if it no longer consists in the representation of a signified by a signifier, is to be traced back to a sort of pure (devoid of any referent, signified, or subjectivity for which it functions) operativity of the order of the signifier alone. This pure operativity engages a second moment in the text: the articulation (soon to prove impossible) of the science of the letter with psychoanalysis.

Indeed, the articulation of the science of the letter with psychoanalysis takes root in the very act of diversion of Saussurean linguistics, if it is the case that "nothing in fact authorizes this diversion except for a certain use of Freud, a certain way of projecting, more or less explicitly, an entire psychoanalytic conceptual framework into Saussurean linguistics in order to disrupt its operation" (*TL.,* 84–85). The nodal point of that articulation is desire; the logic of the signifier becomes a logic of desire. As we saw, in the process of signification, and insofar as the bar forbids any signifier to reach its signified, signifiers can only *slide along* the bar in an indefinite deferral of meaning that Lacan identifies as a "metonymical chain." Even though the metonymical sliding of signifiers ultimately rests upon the abolishment of meaning, this abolished meaning is maintained both as the cause and as the *telos* of the metonymical chain. Insofar as it is lost, it becomes the lacking object of desire; and insofar as it is desired, it is posited as the aim or the end of the chain. This teleological horizon of the chain becomes visible in the very definition of the signifier: as we know, a signifier is what represents a subject *for* another signifier. "For" can be taken as "in place of another," as a substitution of signifiers. But it can also be taken as "*in view* of another," thereby setting into motion a whole "internal teleology of the signifying order" (*TL.*, 75), whose motor is nothing but desire. The metonymical sliding which constituted the very functioning of the signifying order is to be understood in terms of a logic of desire, and desire, in turn, is "constrained by this inaccessible" and "must necessarily follow a metonymical procession and indefinitely defer itself or indefinitely defer its 'end'" (*TL.*, 82). Against the background of the inaccessibility of proper meaning, the letter is related to desire. It is exactly in this motif that Lacoue-Labarthe and Nancy situate the conflation of the science of the letter with psychoanalysis, namely: "in a certain relation *between the letter and truth,* insofar as *desire* is implicated therein" (*TL.*, 82).

If indeed, as Lacoue-Labarthe and Nancy claim, "the logic of the signifier proves to be a logic of desire" (*TL.*, 71), what is at issue is a reinterpretation of the two main axes of language—metaphor and metonymy—in their relation to desire. Metonymy will be recognized as *the trope of desire,* and metaphor as the operation of substitution of one signifier for another or as the moment of abolition of proper meaning, thereby constituting the logic of desire itself, which, as we know, is founded upon a lack. The formula of metonymy, $f(S...S') S \cong S (—) s$, which expresses the maintaining of the bar and the evasion of the signified, is thus read in the following manner: "The 'elided' signified is then able to designate the object of desire as '*lack* of being,' a lack by which desire is doomed to function as a deferral, along the chain, of the metonymy of this lack" (*TL.*, 96). In this way, we understand better how Lacoue-Labarthe and Nancy are able to claim that "metaphor and metonymy, borrowed from Jakobson, have lost their characteristics as complementary 'aspects' of language (whose respective preponderance may vary, according to literary genre, for example) and have become two autonomous entities whose association constitutes the law of language *as the law of desire*" (*TL.*, 114–115, our emphasis).

The moment of articulation thus amounts to a sort of reciprocal, circular relation or exchange, between the texts of psychoanalysis and the science of the letter: for if linguistics was diverted on the basis of the Freudian conceptual apparatus, thus allowing its translation into Freudian terms (metonymy into desire, the bar into censorship, the process of signification into a *Witz*), it is also possible to translate Freudian terms and in particular the different elements of the dream work into linguistic formulations (distortion [*Entstellung*] into the sliding of the signified under the signifier, condensation [*Verdichtung*] into metaphor, displacement [*Verschiebung*] into metonymy, considerations of representability [*Rücksicht auf Darstellbarkeit*] into a system of writing, etc.). As the authors point out, it is strictly impossible to either stop or ground this reciprocal movement; in brief, it is impossible to anchor it in an origin. There is no simple answer to the question: "Who *started* it, Saussure or Freud?" (*TL.*, 85). The lack of origin renders the articulation impossible and makes recourse to a third discourse necessary, the *philosophical.*[8]

This lack of articulation at once disrupts the authors' commentary and directs the text to a question of *strategy*. Their reading becomes a strategic one which follows Lacan's paradoxical reinscription of what his diversion of linguistics had allegedly destroyed. In fact, a genuine sublating (negation and conservation) of the philosophical is at issue in Lacan's discourse, as they point out in the foreword to the third edition.

Diversion, which amounted to a destruction of the metaphysical concept of the sign and introduced a gap or a resistant bar within meaning itself, turns into an encircling movement which encloses what had been displaced. The *movement* of diversion, which the authors define as the combination of all the borrowings, perversions, subversions, repetitions, and ruptures from which Lacan's text is woven, turns itself into a system. That system, which Lacoue-Labarthe and Nancy illustrate in the parodical schema of the circle entitled, after Copernicus, "System" of "The Agency of the Letter," or *De revolutionibus orbium litteralium* (*TL.,* 110), brings the unity of Lacanian discourse into *view,* whatever its disrupting or disruptive elements may be. Indeed, all the main elements of that discourse form a system: "the letter, truth, the Other, being, and the subject form a system here to the extent that the function of each consists of coming to its 'place' *for an other*" (*TL.,* 111). In turn, the circle of the *Agency*, as any circle, has a center. That center is nothing other than the bar itself, where Lacan's discourse is said to "come to a halt on its own sliding," to "center itself" on this stopping; the system of Lacanian discourse centers, anchors, and organizes itself around the *point* of the bar, which here fulfills in every respect the functions of principle, origin, and *archê:*

> The bar is *foundational* or *originary*. It is the *archê* of a system which, while systematizing the division, the lack or the hole in the places of origin, has nevertheless maintained its own '*archaic*' value of systematicity, that is, of origin and center—without questioning it further. (*TL.,* 112)

The subversive power of Lacanian speech, its 'disorganizing' effects, so to speak, are *sublated* into a unitary, centered, systematic discourse, which corresponds to one of the most classical *interests* of philosophical discourse: the achievement of systematicity, the unity or the *archê* and *telos* of a logic. Yet, it is not insignificant to note that Lacoue-Labarthe and Nancy xvi / The Title of the Letter

qualify this "diagnosis" by insisting that diversion, unlike the "importation of concepts," always maintains, in the new context, the diverted elements, always maintains a certain plurality of references. In other words, "the areas of borrowing *do not disappear* from the horizon of the new system" (*TL.,* 89). In this respect, if a system is produced from and through a diverting moment, then it cannot simply be reduced to a *pure* system: "by definition, diversion [is] impure." Again, what is at issue for Lacoue-Labarthe and Nancy is not to locate a simple repetition of philosophical discourse in Lacan's work, but to render a certain ambivalence, or a certain "blurring" (*TL.,* 115), manifest in Lacan's discourse. This is what they do, for example, with respect to the *subject.*

In fact, the motif of the subject was present all along, in particular throughout the diversion of linguistics: for what that diversion accomplished, through the radicalization of the sign, was to accentuate the gap between the level of the statement and the level of enunciation. Now such a distinction can only be relevant for a *speaking subject*: it divides the speaking subject between its "impossible identification" as subject of enunciation and its linguistic representation in a shifter. "The shifter, a singularly remarkable property in linguistics, is thus *diverted* into an irremediable gap between statement...and enunciation, which is the impossible identification of the speaking subject" (*TL.,* 116). Because a subject can only come to be in and through language, that is as *represented* (the order of language is that of the signifier, whose definition is to *represent* a subject for another signifier), it immediately slides under the signifier, or "fades" into it. As speaking subject (that is, as subject of enunciation), it cannot coincide with its being-represented-by-a-shifter (that is, as subject of the statement): "When I say 'I,' this 'I' does not signify *me*" (*TL.,* 70). In brief, a diversion of linguistics, as exemplified in the notion of shifter, produces a subject which is "instituted in and by the signifier" (*TL.,* 70).

This cannot fail, in turn, to dispossess the subject of the privileges that the Cartesian tradition had given it: the trans-

parency to itself and to its own enunciation of self-consciousness, its establishment as master of meaning and language. If
the subject can only come to be in the signifier—as represented,
then, as Lacoue-Labarthe and Nancy state—it can no longer
claim a position from which to repossess itself, as it were, in the
self-transparency of meaning. Truth, as Lacan puts it, can only
be "half-said," and speech is marked by an irreducible split and
alienation. The subject, then, as speaking subject, "is not subjectivity in the sense of being a master of meaning," but rather is
simply the "locus of the signifier" (*TL.,* 64–65). This is a reversal of roles, indeed, in which the so-called Lacanian subversion
of the subject has been located and recognized.

Now, as Lacoue-Labarthe and Nancy point out, if the subject is simply the "locus of the signifier," it literally means that
it is nevertheless "in a *theory of the subject* that the logic of the
signifier settles." It is as if the presence of the subject, however de-centered or ex-centered, faded or lacking, split or alienated, was never put into question. Indeed, it suffices to look at
Lacan's definition of the signifier: "the signifier is that which
represents a subject for another signifier" or "the subject is
that which the signifier represents" (*E.,* 835) to immediately
see that the subject is here, simply, presupposed. It is presupposed in order to be subverted, but presupposed nevertheless.
In this respect, it maintains itself through its very subversion,
not in the sense that it escapes such a subversion, but rather in
the sense that it maintains itself *as* the subverted subject that it
is. The subject is "impossible," "but the signifying order is not
possible without [it]" (*TL.,* 116); the gap of the subject is at
the same time the foundation of the subject; the excentricity
of the subject to itself is undeniable, as the famous Lacanian
statement indicates: "I am not wherever I am the play thing of
my thoughts; I think of what I am where I do not think to
think" (*E.,* 517–18/166). Indeed, Lacoue-Labarthe and Nancy
recognize that such "formulas are indeed statements that displace or dislodge the subject," yet they insist that these formula "nevertheless are enunciations of an *I,* through which this *I*

xviii / The Title of the Letter

conserves the mastery of a certainty which, in spite of its contents, yields nothing to that of the 'I think'" (*TL.,* 120–121). Furthermore, "even the gap of the *shifter* operates almost as a sort of confirmation of the subject adhering to its own certainty through the certainty of its noncoincidence to itself" (*TL.,* 121). Surprisingly, the subversion of the subject never questioned the value of subjectivity itself, which it reinscribed, albeit negatively, thereby producing a sort of *negative* theory of the subject.

The reinscription of the subject as lack allows the authors to diagnose a final sublation of philosophy, that is, of ontology. If Lacan's discourse can be called a negative discourse, or a discourse of *negativity* (that Lacoue-Labarthe and Nancy quickly relate to Hegelian discourse, within which it is, as negativity, always already *comprehended*), then traditional metaphysics (of subjectivity, of meaning, of truth) is not so much destroyed or radically subverted as *inverted* and *displaced* in that very inversion. Lacan's project then continues to inscribe itself in an "ontology," under the guise of a peculiar "onto-theo-semiology"! (*TL.,* 126). But as a *negative* ontology, a hole (the lacking subject, signified) centers it, just as the bar resistant to signification paradoxically centers the production of meaning. The fading of the subject, of its truth and meaning, become *constituting* moments of a negative ontology of the subject, not in the sense that they magically convert the negative into the positive, but rather in that they represent, as the authors assert, in "a gaping hole whose bottom is hidden but whose outline can be discerned" (*TL.,* 126). This is not without precedent, the authors continue, in the tradition of philosophical discourse, for example, as negative theology: "the ultimate effect of Lacanian strategy thus turns out to be a surprising but vigorous repetition of negative theology" (*TL.,* 127).

Although Lacoue-Labarthe and Nancy effectively bring to view certain limits of Lacan's subversion, revealing it more as a *displacement* of a metaphysical conceptuality than its thorough deconstruction, they nevertheless demonstrate that through such a displacement, something happens which exceeds such metaphysical conceptuality. Their reading (in contrast to the seemingly inevitable orthodoxy) thus reopens Lacan's text for further readings.

We have attempted to remain faithful to the nuances and idiosyncracies of the authors. Their highly self-conscious style and close attention to the literality of language—a proliferation of plays on words, alliterations, and explorations of the polysemic resources of the signifier (for example, on the signifier *tree* [*TL.*, 67]) presented quite a challenge. Lacoue-Labarthe and Nancy would not even hesitate, at times, to discuss the polysemy and metaphoricity inherent in their own writing. One such case, discussed earlier, is that of the layers of meaning in the term *title*, as they play in *their* title. Another, is the authors' discussion of the term *agency* [*l'instance*] as it plays in the title of Lacan's text (*TL.*, 22–23). We have attempted, as much as we could, to remain faithful to that letter of their text and render their various plays on words. When this proved impossible, we have maintained the French term or expression in brackets immediately following our translation, or provided an explanatory note.

At times we have translated key terms according to context: for instance, *tour* (which appears in a variety of related expressions, e.g., *re-tournement, dé-tournement, mouvement-tournant, tournure*) appears, alternatively, as "turn," "twist," "play," and even "trick." Some other key terms, on the other hand, required a consistent rendering. With respect to such key terms as well as passages from Lacan, we have generally followed Alan Sheridan's translations. Occasional minor modifications are noted.

One key departure from Sheridan concerns the term *détournement*. Lacoue-Labarthe and Nancy's treatment of this concept, and of how it operates in Lacan's corpus with respect to linguistics, psychoanalysis, and logic, is crucial to their reading. We have chosen to render this term as "diversion." *Détournement* (which has a wide semantic range in French: one speaks of a *détournement d'avion* [airplane highjacking], *détournement de fonds* [embezzlement], *détournement de mineurs* [corruption of minors]) is borrowed by Lacoue-Labarthe and Nancy from Lacan himself who used it in "Subversion of the Subject and the Dialectic of Desire" to designate his treatment of logic. The authors assign a special value to the term *détournement:* the multiple borrowings, perversions, subversions, repetitions, and alterations of various theoretical fields with which Lacan's discourse institutes itself. Elsewhere *détournement* has been rendered in a variety of ways. Alan Sheridan, for example, proposes "distortion" (*E.,* 821/318). This translation, indeed, accurately captures the sense of a subversion or perversion in *détournement.* Lacoue-Labarthe and Nancy, indeed, explicitly identify *détournement* as a gesture of disruption (*TL.,* 85), perversion (*TL.,* 54), subversion (*TL.,* 105), as well as, indeed, destruction (*TL.,* 34). But if "distortion" is accurate in *one* sense, it unfortunately fails to capture *another* sense of the term that the authors emphasize. *Détournement* is indeed a distortion, but in the sense of a *deviation* or *change of course* of the distorted element. This sense is made manifest by Lacoue-Labarthe and Nancy when they qualify Lacan's *détournement* of theory of the sign as a "setting aside" (*TL.,* 63) of the function of the sign in its representative function, or when they underscore its "displacing" effects [Lacan's "critiques" of Saussure are defined, for instance, as "slidings" (*TL.,* 89 and 115), and "gaps" (*TL.,* 115)]. But this is not all. The *distorted* element is *diverted* with the intent of making it enter into a new context. As Lacoue-Labarthe and Nancy explain: "*Détournement*... borrows a concept...in order to make it serve other ends." *Détournement* would then be less a *distortion* than an *appropriation* (or *misappropriation*) of a "borrowed" concept. Indeed, this is what Lacan himself seems to say when he defines his *détournement* of logic in the following terms: "I have indicated to what point I have pushed the *détournement* of the mathematical algorithm *for my own ends.*"[9] It would seem, then, that another, more accurate translation would be "misappropriation," as a recent example suggests.[10] Unfortunately, there is no question of *appropriation,* even less of *misappropriation,* in Lacoue-Labarthe and Nancy's determination of the term *détournement.* First, *misappropriation* has too much of a negative, even pejorative connotation. *Détournement* does not designate anything that could be measured against a norm or propriety. The authors are quite explicit on this point: "There is no basis on which we can reproach Lacan for lacking linguistic rigor"; in fact, Lacan's strategy "evades *critical* jurisdiction" (*TL.,* 115). In this sense, *détournement* evades the simple logic of propriety as well. There is no proper meaning on the basis of which one could judge a *mis*-appropriation. Lacan does not *appropriate,* nor *misappropriate* precisely because *détournement* exhibits a certain excess that evades any proper meaning. A more negative sense of *détournement* in this context would force Lacoue-Labarthe and Nancy into a metaphysical position that they would otherwise seek to avoid. This is why they are careful to contrast *détournement* with the *importation* of a concept: whereas an importation borrows a conceptual unity in order to appropriate it into a new system in a regulated way, *détournement* borrows a concept "without *working* it," that is, leaves room for a certain alterity or polysemy which resists containment and appropriation. *Diversion* [*détournement*] is, as they put it, impure, "an impurity such that it could go as far as to mimic or divert importation itself" (*TL.,* 89). Ultimately *détournement* designates an undecidable "blurring" (*TL.,* 115) which affects Lacan's discourse, a displacing effect which is less the effect of some *intentions* than the excess against which any discourse, including Lacan's, must be measured. That excess is the resource of the ambivalence that Lacoue-Labarthe and Nancy seek to uncover in Lacan's text.

Another key term is *signifiance.* We have chosen not to follow Alan Sheridan in his translation of *signifiance* as "significance," which is too close to *signification,* but have instead left it in the original French.[11] Indeed, the neologism *signifiance*—which Lacan chose in "The Agency of the Letter" to allow him to translate Freud's *Traumdeutung* (*The Interpretation of Dreams*) as *la signifiance du rêve* (*E.,* 519/159)—is specifically distinct from signification. *Signifiance* was forged to account for the signifying operation which is at issue here, and meant to designate the "active, productive sense implied in the present participle on the basis of which the word *signifiant* is formed" (*TL.,* 61). *Signifiance* would then refer, not to signification, but to the very signifying-*ness,* as it were, of the signifying operation, that which (as the prefix *be-* added to form *Bedeutung* indicates) *gives* meaning, *renders* significant. What matters here is that this process is considered from an *operativity* which is "pure."[12] As the authors write unambiguously, "*signifiance* is thus, absolutely, rigorously, and simply not signification itself," but "that which makes signification possible" or even what constitutes it (*TL.,* 62).

Yet, the active and productive sense which determines *signifiance* is paradoxically founded upon the exclusion of the signified, namely on that value which "we could name, in all rigor, *nonsignifying*" (*TL.,* 62). *Signifiance,* Lacan writes, is the operation of the signifier when it has "passed over to the level of the signified" and becomes "charged with signification" (*TL.,* 62). Lacoue-Labarthe and Nancy are quick to point out, however, that this operation of *signifiance* must be considered as an operation against the background of *non-meaning.* The lack of a pregiven signified makes the occurence of signification, in the traditional sense, impossible. Instead, it is only another signifier that *stands in* for a signified, exemplifying the obliteration of any signified as such. The *lack* of meaning becomes, paradoxically, the motor force of the signifying process. It is in this sense that they specify that the value of the signifier is nonsignifying. *Nonsignifying* means, as we know, "being unable to cross the bar." To pass over to the level of the signified, where the process of signification would be produced, then, "is always, and perhaps can only be: to pass *to the limit* of the signified, in other words, *without crossing that limit*" (*TL.,* 62, our emphasis). The authors conclude by insisting that these two theses—that *signifiance* crosses the bar and that *signifiance* only slides along the bar—must be maintained simultaneously. If *signifiance* is an operation against the background of non-meaning or the abolition of proper meaning ("abolition is thus 'non-meaning' and yet it is that which authorizes meaning" [*TL.,* 75]), then it seems inappropriate to follow Sheridan in his translation of the term as "significance."

The translators would like to thank SUNY Press for its support of this project. A number of persons have provided us with important advice at developing stages of the translation. Michael Syrotinski offered crucial guidance in the earliest stages. Edward Casey, David Allison, and Jeffrey Gaines, from the philosophy department at the State University of New York at Stony Brook, offered valuable suggestions throughout the course of the work. In the later stages, essential comments came from Kevin Newmark and Robert Harvey. We are particularly grateful for the attention given to the final manuscript by Gregory Recco, Thomas Blancato, and Stephen Michelman. Finally we would like to thank David's wife Cheri, and his sons Jonah and Ian, as well as Marianne Schoendorff, for their patience and special support.

Notes

1. Jacques Lacan, *Le Séminaire de Jacques Lacan: Livre XX Encore* (Paris: Editions du Seuil, 1975). Hereafter this text will be cited in the Translators' Preface as *XX.*

xxiv / *The Title of the Letter*

2. Hereafter, references to *The Title of the Letter* will be cited as *TL*.

3. Jacques Derrida, in *The Post Card: From Socrates to Freud,* trans., Alan Bass (Chicago: University of Chicago Press, 1987), p. 420.

4. *TL.,* 23, and *Foreword.* The duplication of the title, *The Agency of the Letter in the Unconscious...or Reason Since Freud,* indicates this. Among more recent philosophical readings of Lacan, or readings that interrogate Lacan's relation to philosophy, one may refer to Alain Juranville, *Lacan et la philosophie* (Paris: Presses Universitaires de France, 1984), and to Mikkel Borch-Jakobsen, *Lacan: Absolute Master* (Stanford: Stanford University Press, 1991).

5. For Example, *The Literary Absolute,* trans., Philip Barnard and Cheryl Lester (Albany: State University of New York Press, 1988). Separately, Lacoue-Labarthe has published *Typography,* ed. and trans., Christopher Fynsk (Cambridge: Harvard University Press, 1989) and *Heidegger, Art, and Politics,* trans., Chris Turner (Oxford: Basil Blackwell, 1990), and Jean-Luc Nancy has published *The Inoperative Community* with Minnesota University Press.

6. This would definitely, let us say in passing, delimit or distinguish the Lacanian project with respect to any scientificity. We will return to this diversion of the scientificity of linguistics shortly.

7. On page 840 of his *Ecrits,* (Paris: Editions du Seuil, 1966), Lacan defines the sign as that which represents something for someone. This definition establishes the referentiality of the sign as well as the subject for which there is signification. Henceforth Lacan's *Ecrits* will be cited as *E.* When appropriate, reference to the original *Ecrits* will be immediately followed by reference to the pagination of the English translation, *Ecrits: A Selection,* trans. Alan Sheridan (New York: Norton, 1977).

8. Indeed, the recourse to the philosophical is supposed to settle the undecidability by which the relationship between Freud and Saussure was blocked.

9. *E.,* 821/318–19. Translation slightly modified, our emphasis.

10. Although this is found, one should note, in a polemical text: François Roustang, *The Lacanian Delusion,* trans., Grem Sims (New York: Odéon Press, 1990), p. 97.

11. The OED, however, lists *signifiance* as an obsolete English word.

12. Lacoue-Labarthe and Nancy write on page 49 that, "There is therefore something like a pure *operativity* at the basis of what Lacan himself will later name *signifiance*." "Pure" means pure or devoid of any *reference* to a signified.

Foreword to the Third French Edition

This book was written seventeen years ago. It was first published in 1973 and a second edition appeared that same year which carried no modifications other than a few material corrections. The same holds for this third edition.

Some important considerations, however, could have convinced us to present a new version of a work which is clearly dated in several respects: the passage of time, the history of Lacan's school until its dissolution, the death of its founder, the current diaspora of psychoanalytic groups or institutions as well as the publication of several works devoted to Lacan, particularly to his relation to philosophy.

If we permit the text, however, to appear once again as such, it is not that we judge it to be perfect or to have stood the test of time; quite the contrary. But on the one hand, it seems to us that a text hardly allows for improvement: it calls for others, but it must, for itself, support and confront its own singularity. On the other hand, and above all, the reasons just mentioned for taking it up again are, perhaps, not as compelling as they seemed at first. We must recall, indeed, that the book expressly denied being a book "on Lacan," that is, on Lacanian thought considered as a whole, in the entirety of its theoretical, practical, and institutional phases. Quite clearly, today, a book of this kind could do with what the term "updating" expresses only imperfectly. But only *one* reading of Lacan is in question here, as our subtitle indicated unambiguously. One reading only, and a reading of a single text ("The Agency of the Letter"). It is true that since its first publication, our reading has been considered and used, more than once, as a general discussion or presentation on Lacan. (In fact, Lacan himself contributed to that reception, through the remarks he made about this book in his seminar, since published as *Encore.*) Of couse, on the basis of our reading, one could develop a more general examination of what the signifier "Lacan" denotes. But that was not our intention, and neither were we competent to do so, particularly in regard to Lacan's relation to Freud and psychoanalytic practice.

On the contrary, our intention was quite specific. Through the commentary on and analysis of a text of Lacan—a text chosen or rather discovered by virtue of certain paradigmatic features found at a level where we wanted to operate—it appeared necessary to us to reconstitute a certain philosophical discourse as *one* of the geological strata of Lacan's discourse, and as one of the branches of its genealogy. It seems established today that the philosophical permeates and nourishes a whole part of Lacanian discourse—including the Freudian discourse that Lacan proposed to reformulate (and was the first to do so).

Having granted this, what is however thereby established? Nothing could be less clear. In our intervention, we wished, and still want to contribute toward clarifying the response, or the possible responses to such a question.

Simply observing the play of a certain number of influences, borrowings, or inclusions of so-called philosophical discourse in so-called psychoanalytic discourse would not offer much interest. Such an examination could not be limited to Lacan's psychoanalytic discourse. That discourse, moreover, has the peculiarity of presenting quite a different issue, at least in a text such as "The Agency of the Letter," which actually ends with the dismissal of "centuries of philosophical bravado," and by defining its own object as nothing other that the "question of being."

This issue, whose specificity is still far from being adequately addressed, can be schematized in the following three points:

1. To the extent that Lacan has carried out what is, in fact, a quite singular enterprise of *sublating* philosophical discourse

(whether referred to as "psychoanalytic," "Lacanian," or "of the unconscious"), he has reinvested the dominant values and positions of the philosophical. One must understand *sublation* here in the sense that Derrida gives it when translating Hegel's *aufheben:* to suppress and conserve on another level. In this dialectical operation *par excellence,* Lacan adopted the aims and essential project of the philosophical: the appropriation of a truthful knowledge, systematicity, and the mastery of foundation. He also reproduced and concretized its fundamental political gesture: knowledge is invested with power, decision becomes sovereign, and the communal order is given unitary and authoritarian representation. This explains the well-known succession, in the history of the Lacanian movement, of what today are called "perverse effects" (perhaps, in fact, maliciously authorized by Lacan himself, in view of the final "dissolution," whose meaning for him remains to be considered). Generally, then, it is a question of the sublation of a closed discourse, or more precisely, of the sublation of the closure of that discourse where philosophy, since Heidegger, recognizes and confronts its own end. Psychoanalysis, in turn, might itself succumb to this closure.

2. But if Lacan's discourse indeed lends itself to this interpretation, it nevertheless exceeds it, and our whole reading attempts to make the resources of this ambivalence evident. In another sense, Lacan tries less to sublate philosophy by offering it the truth of a supplementary and final object—the "unconscious"—than he attempts to bring something to light that "works" and disrupts philosophy from its very closure. Under the name of the "unconscious," a name which has been certainly poorly formed and chosen (that Lacan moreover incessantly diverts, at least from its psychological provenance), the question for Lacan is presumably to reassume, in his own way, that constant and more or less hidden movement that takes philosophy to its limits: to the point where the system of the constitution of an object for a subject, the system of representation and certainty, yields to the "archi-constitution"

of "being," whose representation can only be made possible, secondarily, by existence. Essentially, there is no existence "beyond" the world of representation, except in the difference-to-itself of presence in general.

3. However, while pursuing the recognition and exploration of this difference, Lacan tirelessly adapts his discourse, in all sorts of ways, to the possibility of a representation, a true adequate representation of that very thing which challenges and exceeds representation. He does so in different respects by appealing to science, truth, and finally, to the pure locus (in the "Other," or in the "unconscious" itself) of a pure adequation and of a pure presence-to-itself of being in its enunciation: that is the whole ambiguity of "The Agency of the Letter."

We have attempted nothing more than to manifest this ambiguity. With the passage of time it seems increasingly clear to us that it corresponds to the ambiguity in Lacan's work between the daring movement of the invention of a language, of a writing, and the constant desire to found a language of truth—in order to found, on the basis of the latter, a magister and an institution under whose authority a cure could be placed. Lacan knew better than anyone that the psychoanalyst, with "no other authority than his own," risked mimicking the certainty of philosophical subjectivity, and enclosing, if not foreclosing, along with philosophy, psychoanalysis itself. All the same, he more than anyone knew how to speak, by his own authority, from the point where *it* [*ça*] does not speak. But this involves—through him, because of him—the entire history, destiny or fate of psychoanalysis—and this is no longer our concern.

Ph. L.-L./J.-L. N.

Setting the Scene

The following pages only appear in the form of a "book" because they exceeded the limits of publication in a journal. Without a doubt, it is inevitable that this presentation (though by no means *voluminous*) runs at least the risk of producing one of the effects that our culture attaches to a "book" even in (on the basis of?) its materiality—a kind of *binding* effect (of course, in all of its metaphoricity...)—and that might lead one to think that this had the intention of being "a book on Lacan."

We hope, at least, that reading the work will dissipate this impression. There is nothing here that goes beyond—except by indications or suggestions—the exercise of deciphering *one* text of Lacan. Which is to say, in particular, that this specific text is not considered or interrogated outside of the limits of its own situation: first, in the chronology of Lacan's works; but also as to its position or its function as a "theoretical" text, in the sense we will see this term take. This term will refer to the university *address* of the text as well as to the *articulation* of psychoanalytic discourse with scientific and philosophic discourse. This function alone will have legitimized and limited our work.

Moreover, we will see that there is nothing here which presupposes—not even provisionally and despite certain appearances—the idea or horizon of an exhaustive and systematic "interpretation" of Lacan's work. There is nothing, if you will, that aims at the exhaustion or saturation of its meaning (by what right, in what discourse, would we risk it?). Occasional references to Lacan's other texts are intended as nothing more than diverse and dispersed notes. This work has rather been solicited by the *undecidable* of (or in) the question of the "interpretation" of Lacan (that is, at the same time—although not directly—of Freud); and it has remained in that undecidable.

A few empirical remarks should suffice, then, to put these pages "in their place." The first draft was a work presented in the *Groupe de recherches sur les théories du signe et du texte* at the Université des Sciences Humaines de Strasbourg in February 1972. A second draft was presented at a seminar led by Jacques Derrida, at the Ecole Normale Supérieure in May 1972. The final version has only been modified according to the somewhat different conditions of publication.

The two authors have elaborated the text together. If each of them has taken responsibility for the final writing of particular chapters, they have nevertheless written certain passages together, with selective interventions of one "style" into the other when required by the course of the work. In this play of writing, where marked differences are doubtless quite identifiable, one will see that this work is no more *a* "book" than it is a *simple* reading.

But before undertaking this reading, it still remains—because one must after all give in to the law of the genre—to put what serves as the title of this work back in its place: *The Title of the Letter.*

It goes without saying that one *needs* a title. But we know it is hardly possible these days to propose one without bringing to light its semantic richness. And would one resign oneself to choose a title for other reasons? If we have settled on this one, it is indeed because it seemed to offer a certain number of resources. Among others, that of the *title* in the sense that it signifies that document which establishes a right, attests an ownership or capacity—and it is indeed this *title* of the Lacanian letter that it will be necessary to produce, decipher, and authenticate; or further, that of the *title* insofar as it designates the value in gold or silver of a piece of currency—and it is well known that if speech is money, silence is nevertheless golden.

But it also can be read, quite simply, as: *The title: of the let-*

ter—or *on the letter*—which is one way of nullifying our title by letting it become identified with the title of the text we will read.

This is the reason why we will leave this "title" here and (almost) never return to it. And the threshold of this work will be marked by the lone index of its *sub*-title: (A reading of Lacan).

A Turn of Reading

"You prove to me that you have read my Ecrits, *something that people, since they get to hear my lectures, apparently do not deem necessary."*

Lacan, "Radiophonie," *Scilicet* no. 2/3, p. 55

The publication of *Ecrits* has been, as Lacan indicates above, a demand to be read.[1] Now it so happens that, after all, this reading still remains to be done. The time of reading is always late, and that of Lacan does not escape this rule; and even less so because in his case the rule has probably been accentuated by all that which, in and around *Ecrits,* may have converted demand into desire, that is, delayed or forbade the reading itself: the authority of psychoanalysis (which is not without mystery), the founding of an *Ecole,* and finally, the production, or the repetition of these same effects by Lacan's speech.

What will matter here is not the fulfillment of desire—settling the *meaning* of Lacan—but rather attempting to obey the double law by which this "text" offers itself to be read while constantly derailing or deferring the conditions of its reading. At the same time, we hope to show that it is actually impossible to avoid the detour of reading—in the most simple and most patient sense of the term—even if that means overflowing, little by little, its unique and forced course, *reading* itself becoming that very overflowing of the text read in (or by) the reading text.

Such a reading is not without "reasons," even if there can be no simple justification for a gesture which necessarily overflows itself, and first overflows the order and the authority to which traditional *commentary* is submitted (which does have its reasons, if only one, and that reading knows, but is not the only one to know...). This is why we will not hesitate to reveal, as one ought, at least a few of our "reasons"—even if this means pretending to anticipate what will only *turn up* in the course of reading.

Why (and therefore how to) read Lacan? Why (how to) read *a text* of Lacan?

There is no doubt that to read Lacan is first of all to read that discourse by which the question of a genuine relation of psychoanalysis to the "theoretical" order in general has (finally) been raised.

Indeed, prior to Lacan, we know (but we should say that for the most part we owe him that knowledge...) that science and philosophy—or the authorities constituted under these names—divided their "reception" of psychoanalysis between a few traditional attitudes: silence (misrecognition or denial), open hostility, annexation, confiscation, or dedication to the immutable ends of this or that theoretical apparatus. More precisely, nothing has been thought which does not take the form of a "reception," that is to say the subordination of psychoanalysis to a ground, a justification, a truth—that is, most of the time, to a norm.[2]

Freud himself—in spite of his claims as to the revolutionary character of psychoanalysis—kept it essentially in the status of a regional science which is submitted, or ready to be submitted to theoretical jurisdictions other than its own.[3]

Lacan's intervention has consisted in breaking with the system of the "reception," precisely to make psychoanalysis itself intervene in the theoretical field—going so far as to propose something of a new course for the entire configuration of the one and the other, and of the one in the other.

In fact, it was first a question, as we know, of redressing or rectifying psychoanalytic practice, insofar as, once it returned from its exile from Europe, it was following the path of a "reinforcement of the ego"[4] under the aegis of Anglo-American pragmatism and psychologism, that is, following the path of the reinforcement of the resistances of "narcissism" or the sum of its "imaginary identifications," and insofar as its political and social finality was that of the "bleeding heart liberal," European style—in the sense of Jasper's "understanding," and "half-baked personalism."[5]

In order to remove psychoanalysis from this orthopedic function, it was necessary that it be attuned to itself once again. And this is why the practical task implied a theoretical reconstruction. At least this is the way Lacan's discourse establishes itself: according to the system of an articulation of the "theoretical" with the "practical," and according to the movement of a reconstitution of proper identity, through a return to origins.

We know the main features of this establishing: in order to be articulated, Freud's truth required recourse to sciences other than those which seemed to delimit its field (biology and psychology). In order to constitute psychoanalytic discourse in general it was thus necessary to build a whole system of borrowings which appealed to linguistics, structural ethnology, and combinatory logic. Yet, this very procedure rendered necessary the discourse about its own legitimacy, that is, an epistemological discourse—or rather, to the extent it constituted not only a science but a new scientificity, a discourse *on* epistemology. And the whole operation ultimately represented an explicit passage of the psychoanalytic discourse through philosophical discourse—the very passage that Freud never practiced *as such,* even though he always evoked or indicated it implicitly.

Thus we must take this passage into consideration, on the condition, however, that we understand one another.

This does not mean that it is a question of appraising the modalities of this passage in order to evaluate its legitimacy or measure its pertinence. This would imply that we have something like a *truth* of Freud at our disposal. Not only will our reading not be guided by anything of that sort, but it will not even refer to the proper domain of psychoanalysis itself and still less to its practice—or as Lacan calls it, the "clinic."[6] If this is the case, (and this situation is certainly not without paradox), it is no doubt for reasons of competence—but it is also, and first, by virtue of Lacan's very text, and of the philosophical passage (the passage through the philosophical) which takes place therein.[7] The "Freudian truth"—a formula we will return to—does not occur elsewhere than in this very text: one cannot presuppose it, only decipher it. In a way, as we will see, it is only beyond itself that this work will open onto a reading of Freud, and to a much greater extent than it had in fact expected.

One must consequently examine what analysis produces when it passes into the theoretical field, in order to be able to ask about the stakes of an enterprise which presents itself less in a subordination to the "theoretical" than as an *intervention* into the theoretical, from an "outside" which aims to interrogate and challenge [*arraisonner*][8] theory itself.

One could, most certainly, conduct this study on the entirety of Lacan's work—which would amount to presuming a readable or rather visible system as such, apart from the diversity of the texts of which it would be the locus. We will treat of the question of a Lacanian systematicity (at least within *one* piece [*écrit*]), in due time. However, in order to begin our reading, there need be no other assumptions than those of Lacan himself, specifically:

—the will to displace (or overcome?) the systematicity of theoretical discourse in the name of a Freudian revolution imposing "the necessity of humbling the arrogance of all monocentrism."[9] Thus Lacan is able to declare that "[his] statements have nothing in common with a theoretical exposé justified by a closure;"[10]

—the will, consequently, to produce each intervention as an accomplished unity of speech, or of text, which gathers the entire stakes of the work in each enunciation, and defers in the same gesture the totality of statements.

It is thus preferable to read *one* text of Lacan. This means that it is preferable to read, in a sense, *each* of his texts as a focus of concentration and an agency of repetition of all the others; and it is preferable to read *one* text as the singular text that it wants to be, with what such a will cannot fail to connote: the resource of the event, of circumstantial enunciation and therefore, of speech.[11]

What will be at issue is the deciphering of what *happens to* [*arriver à*][12] the theoretical, in a mode which seeks to be novel. The reading will engage a "text," whose proper status and system it at first ignores, and which must be questioned—if indeed it can still be made the object of a question—with respect to its nature as well as its stakes as a text.

In other words, this reading will seek to follow that twist [*tour*] where any "question" of reading is swept away: What are the stakes of Lacan's text (?) —is it even a *text* (?) —in what sense, if we can speak of "sense" here (?) and to what extent?

We will read "The Agency of the Letter in the Unconscious or Reason since Freud."

This text[13] stands out with respect to its date and its circumstances. Delivered and written in 1957, it takes place near the middle of a period during which, between two successive exclusions carried out by the established psychoanalytic societies, Lacan's work produced its most evident disruptions in the field of psychoanalytic practice as well as in psychoanalytic institutions. The same year saw, in the preceding issue of the journal *la Psychanalyse,* the publication of the cardinal text which was to open the *Ecrits:* the "Seminar on the 'Purloined Letter'."[14]

In his *Agency,* Lacan poses this letter (borrowed from Poe for his audience of psychoanalysts) for a university audience composed of the students of the Sorbonne who invited him.[15] Therefore, this is Lacan's first true intervention in the University, in a certain way a symbol—if not the very act—of the passage into the theoretical (should we go so far as to say: theoretical *acting out*?[16]). In "The Agency," psychoanalysis articulates its own theory in the theoretical field considered as such—or rather it articulates itself with theory. We will see how this work must be read as *the text of articulation.*

Such is, in any case, the position that the preamble—which was written for publication—imparts to it. And it is by deciphering briefly the basics of the preamble that we will begin our reading—through this pre-text which is itself Lacan's reading of the *occasion* of his discourse, or the inscription of the discourse in its occasion.

This inscription occurs in a threefold register:

1. "The Agency" is an academic discourse—or at least addressed to academics according to the *universitas* of a certain communication—that of the "necessary generality" (*E.,* 494/147) presupposed as soon as Lacan no longer addresses himself solely to professional analysts. At the same time, the discourse is specified by the "literary qualification" (*E.,* 494/147) of the audience. Thus what the university designates as *humanities* [*lettres*], and in particular as literature will prove suited to the Lacanian elaboration of the "letter."

2. It is at the same time a scientific discourse—or at least, and more broadly, a discourse held in the order of knowledge, with the aim of being a discourse on a certain *truth.* In any case it is a discourse of a certain "veracity." In the preface of his address, Lacan immediately dismisses *bad* (*false*) received knowledge, in particular the ethnolinguistics of Sapir and Jespersen: his avowed goal is the denunciation and refutation of any "false identity" (*E.,* 494/147) of psychoanalysis.

3. Consequently, this discourse is *also* a discourse for psychoanalysts (and, as such, a "training" discourse) but only through the mediation, if you will, of the two other discourses. This mediation gives the occasion of his discourse, the "expediency" of which Lacan was aware, its entire weight. The *"universitas litterarum,"* where a certain knowledge of the

humanities is communicated, is the place Freud intended for the preliminary training of the analyst, and it is from this place that the discourse can claim to exhibit "the true" identity (*E.,* 494/147) of psychoanalysis.

What is principally at stake, then, is a discourse attending to the demands of the *universitas* and of science. Lacan's text inscribes itself as a *discourse,* within and between its lines. If Lacan was able to say, "I always place buoys by which one can navigate in my discourse,"[17] this is because it is possible—if not easy—to find the point and itinerary of the concept (of the properly conceptual procedures, importations, or productions).

Is it not somewhat paradoxical that this text, a text devoted to the subversion of the "classical" authority of discourse, should itself reconstruct another classical discourse? Even so we still have to read this paradox. To this end we cannot shrink from an academic reading, that is, a *commentary* with all the heavy, unrewarding, reductive, exhausting aspects it may have with respect to the most salient effects of Lacan's teaching. At least in this way we can be sure that its most decisive determinations will not be overlooked either through excess or default.

Lacan's "text," then, finds its primary status for us in this system, which suits the formula and form [*tour*] of the "textual commentary." This is why we will begin by commenting on the first part of the exposé ("The Meaning of the Letter"), where the theory of the letter is established.

But beyond this commentary, the point will be to decipher what can only appear as a *repetition* of the first part in the two following parts ("The Letter in the Unconscious" and "The Letter, Being, and the Other"), a repetition destined to allow the articulation of the theory of the letter with psychoanalysis itself. This is, as we will see, the articulation of Saussure and Freud, which is itself articulated, in the last analysis, on yet another level—or by another character, another proper name, which will appear in time. Our reading will consequently complicate its form [*tour*] in accordance with this play of repetition and articulation.

This means that it will have to deal, in particular, with what Lacan's preamble sets forth as the twofold or mixed character of his address.

In effect, Lacan tells us, his address is not "writing" for writing "is distinguished by a prevalence of the *text*," and the *text*—that "purveyor of discourse" [*facteur du discours*], which remains suspended between the postman and the mathematical parameter and whose "meaning" is promised by the lecture itself—is itself specified by a "tightening up...which leaves the reader no other way out than the way in" (*E.*, 493/146). One understands, to the extent that the "text" allows, that the word *text* here includes the sense of the ideal (of the absolute) of *discourse,* in the constraining necessity of its conceptual process and in the remainderless circularity that results from it—and that this ideal must not "prevail."

The address will thus be between "writing and speech," for the latter's "different techniques are essential to the formative effects I seek" (*E.*, 494/146). Consequently, it will be necessary to read that which, halfway between the two, diverges from the text and disrupts it. It will be necessary to read *between* hearing (the discourse) and reading (the text). For our reading, Lacan's *text,* or at least what we will interrogate as such, in the "strong" sense of the word (but precisely here in the sense least determinable by a discursive logic of meaning), will have to be sought in that gap, or as that semi-absence which emerges in the process of reading between the lines—or rather between sentences. More exactly, perhaps, the question of the *text* will have to become that of the gap or of the non-gap, in Lacan's address, between discourse as heard (as understood, as deciphered, or perhaps as believed) and the text as read.

Our commentary, *in turn*—a reconstruction and transcription in a resolutely manifest discourse—will of course have to be destroyed.[18] We did not submit to its movement simply to resign ourselves to it, and it is by "working" the results of the commentary in order to exceed (in every sense of the word) its status that the reading, by submitting to the complex motif of the "Lacanian text," must be risked—without us being able to indicate in advance what *twist* [*tour*]—that is, what *text*—such a destruction could produce, nor whether it will occur *because of* or *despite* Lacan's text, or according to some other more complicated figure.

In this process, we will finally have to recognize that our reading must consequently go through the deciphering of a certain play of *metaphor* in Lacan's text. It is precisely that metaphor which, in the epigraph of the preamble (*E.,* 493/146), governs, from the outset, the entire text of *The Agency.*

Borrowed from de Vinci's *Prophesies,* this epigraph belongs to a collection of texts—of a conventional genre—whose titles constantly function as metaphors of the content of the prophesies. Here the "children in swaddling clothes" metaphorize a servitude, itself marked by the enslavement of one language to another, which reduces the first to the partial muteness of a "language" of passions. The prophesy is thus, for Lacan, a metaphor or an allegory of *both* the unconscious as language *and* of the social (and psychoanalytic—in the sense of psychoanalytical cures of "false identity") repression of this very unconscious—or even of the truth which Freud's and Lacan's work articulates.

The address establishes that the unconscious only produces its "meaning" in metaphor. Thus Lacan's text guards itself, in the epigraph, against that which it must exhibit and work. The traditional situation and function of an epigraph is that it only becomes readable in the course of the text. But that this readability leads us back to the very (metaphorical) functioning of the epigraph, or to a *literality of metaphor,* is what seems to seal the course of Lacan's discourse *in* this very trope. Consequently, the last "state" of Lacan's "text," which will command the last turn of reading, will have to be this sort of generalized metaphoricity, or identification with (and of) metaphor.

For now, we will simply take the occasion to inscribe the epigraph of our reading, without yet giving a verdict on its functioning:

We are obliged to operate with the scientific terms [*Termini*] that is to say with the figurative language proper ["*die eigene Bildersprache*"] to psychology (or more precisely to depth psychology). We could not otherwise describe the processes in question at all, and indeed we could not have become aware of them. The deficiences of our description would probably vanish if we were already in a position to replace the psychological terms by physiological or chemical ones. It is true that they too are only part of a figurative language, but it is one with which we have been long familiar and which is perhaps a more simple one as well.[19]

It is presumably possible now, to begin reading (again).

The first moment, that of the commentary—if we can borrow a formula which was produced elsewhere with the aim of naming the Lacanian theory as a whole,[20] will be that of *a logic of the signifier.*

Notes

1. Cf. as well in *Scilicet* no. 1 (Seuil, 1968), "La méprise du sujet supposé savoir," and "Raison d'un échec."

2. Of course one must exclude from this evocation those already engaged in a subversion of theoretical authority as such, whatever their relations to psychoanalysis might have been: above all, Georges Bataille, whose name will appear in our reading.

3. No doubt this is only Freud's most *manifest* discourse, and furthermore the effects of a certain deliberate *prudence* in that discourse itself. But we are not undertaking here to *read* Freud.

4. "La psychanalyse et son enseignement," *Ecrits,* p. 454. Cf., the entirety of this text. The references to the *Ecrits* refer to the

complete edition published by Seuil (collection "Le champ freudien") in 1966. They will henceforth be noted as *E.*, and will not be footnoted when they concern the text we are reading: everything that follows assumes that one could reread that text at any time.

T.N. Page references to the original *Ecrits* will be immediately followed, when appropriate, by reference to the pagination of the English translation edition, Jacques Lacan, *Ecrits: A Selection,* trans., Alan Sheridan (New York: Norton, 1977).

5. "La science et la vérité," *E.*, p. 867.

6. This is the proper limit of our reading which was set in place earlier. Thus nothing will be prejudged with respect to Lacan's more specifically "clinical" discourse. We will only decipher what subsequently makes possible (according to a procedure which remains to be analyzed) the determination of the "clinical" in and through the theoretical discourse, the theory of psychoanalysis and psychoanalysis as theory. But it goes without saying—given, precisely, the comprehensive stakes of the Lacanian operation—that this limit is not one in the sense that we would only "treat" "one aspect" of that operation. If the pure jurisdiction of the theoretical must be blurred, neither must we recognize its *alter ego:* what would seek to present itself as the pure authority of the "practical" in itself.

7. This is how Lacan himself specifies his *Ecrits* in relation to his teaching as a whole: they "seek to pin down the essential subject matter of the seminars," and "what is more they introduce what is essential in this material in the context of an epistemological critique of the curent psychoanalytic view on the domain being studied." [An interview with Jacques Lacan in A. Rifflet-Lemaire's *Jacques Lacan,* trans., David Macey (Boston: Routledge and Kegan Paul, 1977), p. 252].

8. T.N. *Arraisonnement* is how some French translators of Heidegger have rendered *Gestell.* It includes the sense of putting something in question.

9. "Radiophonie," *Scilicet* no. 2/3, p. 73.

10. In an interview with Rifflet-Lemaire, *Lacan*, p. 252.

11. The locus of Lacan's discourse is the seminar, and not the "written": we will have the opportunity to insist on this again. When we speak about Lacan's *discourse,* one must always understand both the theoretical determination of the locus as well as the link of con-

cepts, and "discourse" in the linguistic sense of "extended speech." (Cf. R. Barthes, *Elements of Semiology,* trans., Annette Lavers and Colin Smith (New York: Hill and Wang, 1968), p. 15.

12. T.N. *Arriver à* can mean either "to arrive at," "to reach," or "to happen." Consequently it means here both what arrives at the theoretical as well as what happens to the theoretical.

13. Which Lacan recalled later several times with a certain insistence. Cf. in particular "Radiophonie," and "Lituraterre" in *Litérature,* no. 3 (Larousse, 1971), p. 5: "Could it be a dead letter that I put in the title of one of those pieces I have called *Ecrits...*"The Agency *of the Letter,*" as reason of the unconscious?" Let us indicate very briefly that this is not a reason to privilege this piece of writing. In several respects, other writings are no doubt as least as important in the Lacanian apparatus (for example, "Seminar on 'The Purloined Letter,'" "The Signification of the Phallus," and "The Subversion of the Subject"). Still, these texts are hard to read with respect to the discourse that underlies them without the *The Agency.* Moreover, our reading applies to *The Agency's* theoretical *property* (and not to its theoretical "privilege")—to the proper turn that the theoretical takes there.

14. This text, issued from a 1955 seminar, carries however, as Lacan notes, the marks of the theory as was elaborated at the time of its writing, which slightly precedes that of *The Agency.*

15. Cf. *E.,* 908.

16. T.N. "*Acting Out*" in English in the original.

17. *Radiophonie,* Scilicet no. 2/3, p. 13.

18. As for the *commentaries* which have been produced on Lacan up to now, one should say, at least, that they have remained unaffected by the "text" they set out to interpret or repeat. It goes without saying that we do not speak here of those texts or essays which, while expressly presenting themselves under Lacan's constant authority, if not as a "repetition" of his themes, still did not claim to be commentaries: for example, "De la structure en psychanalyse," by M. Safouan, in *Qu'est-ce que c'est le structuralisme?* (Seuil, 1968).

19. Sigmund Freud, *Beyond the Pleasure Principle* (1920), trans., James Strachey, *The Standard Edition of the Complete Psy-*

chological Works of Sigmund Freud (London: Hogarth Press, 1953), XVIII, 60, translation slightly modified). Henceforth Freud's *Standard Edition* will be cited as *S.E.,*.

20. J.-A. Miller—"La suture. Elements pour une logique du signifiant," *Cahiers pour l'analyse,* no. 1. Except for its brevity, this formula follows Lacan to the letter: cf., for example, *E.,* 468 and 469.

Part I

The Logic of the Signifier

Since the point now is to *decipher,* we may as well begin by tackling the subtitle of the first part: "The meaning of the letter."

No doubt we should first understand this subtitle in several senses, that is (even if it must seem a little forced), according to the meaning that one could give to the word *meaning* [*sens*] and, of course, to the meaning [*valeur*] that one could attribute to the genitive. For example, to stress the point: *the signification of the concept of the letter,* or else *the meaning that the letter produces* (if not: *the meaning that the letter is*), or, moreover, *to have a sense* [*sens*] *of the letter* as one has "business sense." But it is also indispensable, obviously, to relate it to the general title: "The Agency of the Letter in the Unconscious or Reason since Freud," of which it is but the first application.

Undertaking a commentary of a title always presupposes the completion of the reading of the text it governs. It is thus out of the question to risk it, even as a tactical device. But since it is nevertheless at least necessary to situate the text we have to read (this being a classical rule), we will allow ourselves two preliminary remarks with respect to the title:

1. The first will concern the use of the word, or of the concept, *agency*—it being understood, if we may anticipate a little, that speaking of concept will henceforth require a certain number of precautions, since, for Lacan, the concept may turn out to be constructed, as it is here, on a play on words (not to mention: on his word play). Indeed, we know that according to the *Littré Dictionary,*[1] agency [*instance*] originally designates a *pressing solicitation* (one insistently requests), an *argument* or even a *trial,* (insofar as a trial presupposes accusation and defence and, consequently, a clash of arguments). Hence, by extension, the meaning established, in classical language, of a *judicial authority* (one says: a judge or a court of first instance [*tribunal d'instance*]). However, in modern usage, this specifici-

ty of the term has been lost and one hardly ever uses the word *agency* except in the very general sense of an *authority with decision-making power* (a sense, moreover, that Littré ignores and Robert presents as a neologism). The agency of the letter is thus the authority of the letter. Moreover, if it is the case that the first sense [*sens*] of the Latin *instare* (*to be above*) still resonates as an echo in the contemporary usage—which is not necessarily a misusage—that sense [*valeur*] is further reinforced and the title would here point to the domineering position of the letter, the exalted place that it occupies and from which it derives its decision-making power and its authority, and from which, in other words, it rules and legislates. But we must also take account of the possibility of a *Witz,* of a *witticism: agency* [*instance*] indeed is almost like *insistence* (short of a syllable, which is that of the frequentative). Moreover, in its first sense, to *insist* is *to make a stand* [*faire instance*], *to demand insistently.* Nowhere, to our knowledge, is the word explicitly emphasized by Lacan.[2] We will see however that *insistence* appears in this very text (*E.,* 502/153) and we know that it is indeed a major concept of Lacanian discourse: the concept by which the specificity of the *signifying chain* is marked as the imminence or indefinite deferral of meaning that is the basis of the repetition compulsion—Freud's *Wiederholungszwang.*[3] In this sense, the agency of the letter could perhaps also be its insistence—something like the suspension of meaning. This does not fail to complicate, as we suspect, the interpretation of the subtitle of the first part.[4]

2. The second remark we would like to make concerns the duplication of the title: "The Agency of the Letter...*or* Reason since Freud." This is a quite traditional duplication that, presumably, is also quite parodical. It is in any case a duplication which calls our attention to the sliding of meaning that it may occasion (in a premeditated manner). The duplication indicates at least this: Since Freud, since a certain break or a certain rupture that took place with Freud, reason is no longer what was previously understood by this word, but rather the

agency (or insistence) of the letter in the unconscious. This means two things: reason is the letter *and* hence what passes *in* and *through* the unconscious (the stylistic effect intended here is clearly that of antithesis in the rhetorical sense of the word). Even in jest, this "specification" confirms in any case what we have already been able to read, in passing, in the preamble: that this text is proposed straightaway and openly as a *philosophical* text. A certain aim of the unconscious, of what predominates in it and as such determines it, as well as the taking into account of the letter and what is at stake there regarding meaning, all this concerns the definition of reason in general, *ratio* or *logos*. It is in sum, this event, this mutation or upheaval that the text takes for its object.

We will begin the commentary on the first part from the perspective opened by the double play of the title and the subtitle. For convenience of exposition and because it is a question, as in any commentary, of attempting to reconstitute a logic in order to lay out its structure (we will see to what extent this is possible…), we will propose a rough four part division of the text corresponding to its most visible articulations. At the same time we will give a title to each of these parts (which will indicate less their object than what we are trying to read into them).[5]

The first of these parts occupies the first two pages of the text, from page 495/147 to the first paragraph on page 497/149. We will entitle its commentary: "the science of the letter."

Notes

1. T.N. Here and hereafter "Littré" and "Robert" refer respectively to Emile Littré's *Dictionnaire de la Langue Française* [*Dictionary of the French Language*] (Paris: Gallimard/Hachette, 1966–7), and Paul Robert's, *Dictionnaire Alphabétique et Analogique de la Langue Française* [*Alphabetical and Analogical Dictionary of the French Language*] (Paris: Société du Nouveau Littré, 1978).

2. Except for recently in "Lituraterre" (in *Littérature,* no. 3, October 1971, p. 5).

3. Cf. for example: *E.,* 11/*P.,* 38, *E.,* 557/200. T.N. The citation *P.,* refers here, and henceforth, to the English translation of "Seminar on 'The Purloined Letter,'" in John P. Muller and William J. Richardson, eds., trans. Jeffrey Mehlman (Baltimore: The Johns Hopkins University Press, 1988).

4. All this could indeed be maintained on the condition that one does not forget that one year earlier (in 1956), Benveniste had proposed the concept of an "agency of discourse" in order to designate the "discrete and each time unique acts by which language is actualized in speech by a speaker" (*Problems in General Linguistics,* trans., Mary Elizabeth Meek [Florida: University of Miami Press, 1971], p. 217). Now this definition served precisely, we know, to direct the analysis of "the nature of pronouns," in which the theory of enunciation and of the "indicators" of discourse was constituted, in hommage to R. Jakobson who was to reformulate it later ("les Embrayeurs...," in "Shifters, Verbal Categories, and the Russian Verb," in *Roman Jakobson: Selected Writings* v. II [The Hague: Mouton, 1971], p. 134)—we will return to this later. But one will not forget that for Aristotle, ἕνστἄσις, in the theory of refutation, designates the *obstacle* which one opposes to the reasoning of an adversary (*Rhetoric,* II, 25, 1402a); cf. *Prior Analytics* II, 26, *Topics,* VIII, 2, 157ab. This "agency" is, in particular, what the exception opposes to a universal predication. An example of this *topos* happens to be the following, to be appreciated according to its most "proper" meaning: "...it is honorable in some places to sacrifice one's father, for example amongst the Triballi, but it is not honorable in an absolute sense" [*Topics* II, 11, 115b, trans., E. S. Furster, in Aristotle's *Organon* (Cambridge: Harvard University Press, 1960), translation slightly modified].

5. Though Lacan does not allude to it, one might also wonder if *agency* could be taken in the sense that Quine gives it. It would thus be a question—in the most simple and general sense—of that or those propositions which could be substituted by a *letter* used as a symbol in the calculus (of symbolic logic): "Any statement is the instance of any letter." (Quine, *Elementary Logic* [Cambridge: Harvard University Press, 1966], p 39). Lacan's title could be deciphered as the proposition (the statement, the discourse) which, in the unconscious, is the *agency* of a *letter,* a letter which is not just any symbol, but *the* letter, or literality itself (the symbolic itself). The

entire text could then be taken as a diversion of logic, to which we will have to return. (Let us add that Quine's use of the term is itself due to the retention, more visible in English than in French, of the senses included in the *instantia* of the scholastics: an example that supports a claim; an instrument of proof or manifestation in general; a sign or mark.)

1.

The Science of the Letter

This science will certainly not be constituted straightaway. It will first require the definition of its object (this is the object of these two pages), namely, the concept of *letter*. As we reconstitute this definition schematically, we could propose the following:

1. First, the letter essentially designates *the structure of language insofar as the subject is implicated therein.* Whatever its modalities, this implication is not only initial but is the foundation of the entire logic which will be set up. To say that the letter is what implicates the subject means, even before "taking the letter to the letter " (according to the expression on page *E., 495/147*, translation modified), taking the subject *in* the letter—which will soon appear, as one might expect, as a way of taking the subject to the letter.

This *literalization* of the subject is twofold. On the one hand, "the structure of language exists prior to the entry that the subject makes there at a certain moment of its mental development" (*E.,* 495/148). This explains the reference to Jakobson and specifically the use of his well-known text on aphasia[1] since, although its cause may very possibly be entirely anatomical, aphasia is more fundamentally determined according to the structure of language, that is to say, nonanatomically and in such a way that the agency, here, is that structure itself— or this is at least what Lacan retains for now.

On the other hand, literalization stems from the fact that as a speaker, the subject borrows the *material support of its discourse* from the structure of language. Lacan writes: "By letter we designate that material support that concrete discourse borrows from language" (*E.,* 495/147). Two concepts are at stake here: First, the concept of *concrete discourse,* which is determined by its relation to both language as a structure and to speech (in the Saussurean sense, as the individual performance of language) in order to retain the element common to both. In turn, this element is twice specified (and here we will borrow a few formulations from the text "Function and Field of Speech and Language in Psychoanalysis") as "intersubjectivity of speech" in interlocution, and "transindividuality" of language (and of the subject): "its means," Lacan says of psychoanalysis, "are those of speech, insofar as speech confers a meaning on the functions of the individual; its domain is that of concrete discourse, insofar as this is the field of the transindividual reality of the subject." (*E.,* 257/49).

The second concept at stake is that of *material support.* We will refer here to two texts: on the one hand, "The Seminar on 'The Purloined Letter,'" where, on the basis of the letter (the missive) which gives Poe's story its title and which is hidden, we recall, in a place so evident that no one sees it, Lacan defines the *materiality of the signifier* in two ways: as the signifier's ability to be located, its "relation to place" (*E.,* 23/*P.,* 38)—but this localization is always, strangely, a "being-out-of-place," [*un manque à sa place*] if place designates a location in objective reality—and as its indivisible character. This localization and indivisibility consequently lend an *odd* materiality to the signifier. This materiality is itself odd in that it is *unquantifiable* (*E.,* 23,24/*P.,* 38, 39). On the other hand, "Function and Field of Speech...," where, on the basis of the question of the relation of language to the body, language is defined as not being immaterial ("It is subtle body," Lacan states, but body it is"), a definition which justifies itself as much from certain kinds of somatic forms, including, for example, hysterical ones ("Words are trapped in all the corporeal images that captivate the subject; they may make the hysteric pregnant and can be identified with the object of *penis-neid*," etc.) as from the possibility for words to "undergo symbolic lesions," to "accomplish imaginary acts of which the patient is the subject" (*E.,* 301/87) (as for example in *The Wolf Man,* where the word *Wespe* [*wasp*] is castrated of its initial W, becoming precisely the initials S. P. of the subject).

To say that the letter is the material support that concrete discourse borrows from language means (under these conditions, that is under the condition of taking account of the displacement to which Lacan subjects each of these terms): on the one hand (according to a classical formulation) the subject, during the act of elocution (which is the act of relation to others), draws from the constituted material that language provides for it; and on the other hand, the subject only enters into transindividuality insofar as it is already implicated in a discourse which is itself supported or determined by the agency of this odd materiality of the letter.

The emphasis placed on materiality is thus at least the sign of a twofold refusal: a refusal to assign an origin to language, either in the ideality of meaning or in its mere reversal, a somatic materiality, for example. Thus it is neither idealism nor materialism, although the emphasis is placed, after it has been distorted [*gauchi*], on the second of these two terms. This twofold refusal, which engages the entire linguistic determination of the unconscious, will be moreover the corollary of another refusal relative to the status of the unconscious itself. The unconscious will not be seen as the seat of the instincts. If it is a question, then, of a materiality of language as well as of the unconscious, this materiality is not to be conceived as a *substantial* materiality, at least according to what classical materialism is said to claim. The letter is matter, but not substance. This unqualifiable term, apparently irreducible to any of the oppositions of traditional philosophic conceptuality, will assume the "major place" (if one can still speak of it in this way) in what, since Freud, is called "the unconscious."

2. But this theory of the letter also engages, in a second

moment, the preinscription of the subject in discourse, through its proper name:

> Thus the subject too, if it appears the slave of language is all the more so the slave of a discourse in the universal movement in which its place is already inscribed at birth if only by virtue of its proper name. (*E.,* 495/148, translation slightly modified.)

This preinscription radicalizes what has already been recognized as the implication of the subject in language. It reinforces its literalization. The subject of concrete discourse is not only enslaved to language as structure, but antecedently to the actualization of language in discourse itself. For there is no subject according to Lacan which is not always already a *social* subject, that is, a subject of communication in general, which Lacan describes in terms that are ultimately quite close to those of the classical discourse of philosophical anthropology. The subject of communication is indeed the subject of a contract by which speech is guaranteed. Thus, in the third part of the text ("The Letter, Being, and the Other") (where it will be a question of defining the Other (with a capital O), whose discourse is the unconscious, that is, of uprooting the subject of the unconscious from any identity to itself and even from any simple alterity, in order to define it in its radical "excentricity" and "heteronomy"), Lacan, while following the Hegelian dialectic of desire, conflict, and recognition fairly closely, as he often does, will distort its process and disrupt its effects by a simultaneous recourse to game theory and to contract theory. This would make recognition appear as the recognition of speech, which does not presuppose the Other as an origin but rather as the very rule of the functioning of language, by which language can be determined in its twofold function of truth and falsehood. Thus the subject will be installed by the Other in the midst of language as "signifying convention" (*E.,* 525/173), whose rules will determine the place of the subject itself and guarantee the truth of its speech, even if false—since falsity is in no way animalistic, nothing that could be reduced to a natural cunning in service of need.

Therefore literalization refers as well to a theory of contract and to the conventional passage from animality to humanity. We are dealing, if you will, with a Rousseauism, but with the difference that the well-known difficulty of the second *Discourse* in regard to the anteriority of language or of the civil state would be here settled in favor of language, and hence nullified. This is moreover what the passage which concerns us clearly emphasizes: the second enslavement of the subject, which consists in its nominal preinscription, is not founded on the anteriority of community or of society in relation to the individual, but rather on the anteriority of language in relation to the individual. The sociality of the Lacanian subject blends with the radical primitiveness of the letter. Therein lies its literality. Hence the recourse to the concept of an originary, founding *tradition,* anterior to history itself and produced by discourse (*E.,* 496/148). Hence, still, the implicit reference, in the second paragraph of this same page, to Levi-Strauss, that is to the displacement of the former nature/society opposition into the nature/society/culture tripartition, where culture, reduced to language, has the specific responsibility to insure the partition of nature and society. Hence finally, the allusion to the Soviet debate concerning the superstructurality of language, which was settled, as we know, by Stalin.

These points aim together to refute any ethnolinguistic reorientation of the theory of the subject, but we also understand now that all this contractualism is meant only to prepare the installation of the theory of the subject within the only science that will be suitable for it.

This science, one suspects, is the science of the letter. But the fact that it is to be grounded does not mean it has no origin, nor even that it is not, in a way, already constituted. The science of the letter is not, in fact, without relation to linguistics, at least insofar as the theory of the subject must go through a theory of language. This is why we can consider that this first part ends on Lacan's appeal to the Saussurean foundation of linguistics as science. This appeal is formulated in the very terms of contemporary epistemology, that is, both in the evocation of the experimental status of linguistics which guarantees the scientificity of its object, (*E.,* 496/148) and in the application of the Bachelardian concept of *break* to the founding gesture of Saussure.[2] One must thus adjust a theory of the subject which has no relation to any anthropology or psychology to this "emergence" of linguistics, which is a "revolution of knowledge" insofar as it declassifies and reclassifies all sciences, unless we are dealing with the opposite movement, and find that it is from the displacement introduced by linguistics that another science of the subject must be produced. This reciprocity is, for the moment, impossible to undo, except to note, if we are to follow step by step the movement of this text, that it is indeed on the basis of linguistics that the science of the subject proceeds, progressively constituting itself.

This is what we will attempt to reconstruct in a second part—between pages 497/149 and 501/153 in the text—which we have entitled: "algorithm and operation."

Notes

1. Roman Jakobson and Morris Halle, "Two Aspects of Language and Two Types of Aphasic Disturbance," in *Fundamentals of Language* (The Hague: Mouton, 1980).

2. Lacan's allusion (p. 496–7/149) presumably refers to a combination of the concepts of *recasting* and *break* as we find them in Bachelard's work.

2.

Algorithm and Operation

The task is thus to seek the science of the letter in Saussure's linguistics.

From the concept of epistemological break to which he has referred implicitly, Lacan retains that element according to which a science cannot institute itself by the mere treatment of a novel empirical object, but by the prior determination of a calculative mode (and of a corresponding conceptuality) on the basis of which alone an object of science can be constructed.

Lacan interprets that determination as the founding position of an *algorithm*.

> To pinpoint the emergence of linguistic science we may say that, as in the case of all sciences in the modern sense, it is contained in the constitutive moment of an algorithm that is its foundation. (*E.*, 497/149)

But to use this term is, at least, to extend all the concepts of Bachelardian epistemology. Indeed, if the algorithm designates, in its first sense, a procedure of algebraic calculus, we know that it designates, in its modern sense, a procedure of differential notation. More precisely, the algorithm designates a procedure that is constitutive of a logic for which, as we know, the two expressions *algorithmic logic* and *symbolic logic* are equivalent.

One sees, then, in what sense one is able to speak here of extension: extension by virtue of an overflowing of the limits of the strictly mathematical domain. Unless of course one takes *algorithm* here as a *concept* in the epistemological sense (as defined, for example, in Canguilhem's work). In that case, it would simply be the concept of *sign,* which could very well be that which institutes linguistics as a science. But then the notation Lacan proposes,

$$\frac{S}{s}$$

would be nothing but a formal, that is to say, economical notation of the concept of the sign. Now Lacan does indeed speak of *formalization (E.,* 497/149), in the modern sense, insofar as it makes a logical calculus possible. Furthermore, it is apparently a calculus that is at issue in the second part ("The Letter in the Unconscious"), where the formulas of metaphor and metonymy are established (*E.,* 515/164). We must, therefore, take *algorithm* in the strict sense.

We will see, in fact, that it is essentially a question of subjecting the Saussurean sign to a certain *treatment.* To algorithmize the sign, if we can risk this expression, will practically mean to prevent it from functioning as a sign. We could even say that as it is posited, it is destroyed.

Indeed, with regard to the algorithm, Lacan says that "it should be attributed to Ferdinand de Saussure although it is not found exactly in this form in any of the numerous schemas that appear in [the]...*Course in General Linguistics (E.,*497/ 149). This is a *coup de force,* or as Lacan says, a "homage," which derives its authority from the fact that Saussure's teaching is "a teaching worthy of his name, which one can only come to terms with in its own terms" (*E.,* 497/149).

One indeed finds the following schema in Saussure's work, which is probably the closest to the Lacanian algorithm:[1]

If we compare it to the algorithm, we will notice that the signifier appears *under* the bar (moreover, all of Saussure's schemas are identical in this respect), and that, even if we take the symbolization attributed to Saussure by Barthes into account:

$$\frac{\text{Sa}}{\text{Sé}}$$

which also reverses the Saussurean schema (although Barthes interprets it in strictly Saussurean terms), in fact we never really encounter anything but a procedure of convenient notation.[2] On the other hand, four principal features distinguish the algorithm:

1. The disappearance of a certain parallelism between the terms inscribed on both sides of the bar, since, as Lacan indicates, we must not read merely "signifier over signified," but "capital S" over "small *s*" (the latter being written, moreover, in italics).

2. The disappearance of the ever present Saussurean ellipse which, as we know, symbolizes the structural unity of the sign.

3. The substitution of the two *stages* of the algorithm for the Saussurean formulation of the two *faces* of the sign.

4. Finally, the emphasis placed on the bar separating S from *s*. (The algorithm indeed reads: "signifier over signified, the *over* corresponding to the bar which separates the two stages.")

This is, moreover, what Lacan himself takes up in his commentary on this algorithm:

> The thematics of this science is henceforth suspended, in effect, at the primordial position of the signifier and the signified as being distinct orders separated initially by a bar resisting signification. (*E., 497/149*)

But only to add immediately:

> And that is what was to make possible an exact study of the connections proper to the signifier, and of the extent of their function in the genesis of the signified. (*E., 497/149.*)

Thus, not only does the positing of the two distinct orders of signifier and signified harden an opposition which is no doubt present in Saussure's work, although it is always rectified by the notion of a constitutive relation of the sign in its indissociability (this is, for example, the well-known image of the front and back of the same page, or else the inverted double arrows which in most cases frame the schema of the sign[3]); but more radically, the separation of these two orders by a bar which resists signification disrupts the Saussurean concept of the sign through and through. Whereas for Saussure, what is essential is the *relation* (the reciprocity, or the association), Lacan introduces a resistance such that the crossing of the bar, the relation of the signifier to the signified, in short, the production of signification itself, will never be self-evident. Thus, the displacement carried out with respect to Saussure does not *first* and *simply* depend, as is too often said, on the autonomization of the signifier. The autonomy of the signifier is real, but not primordial. It depends on the resistance itself—and from one paragraph to the next, the text we just cited indicates this explicitly. What is primordial (and foundational) is in fact the bar. The division by which the science of the letter is instituted is finally nothing other than the division introduced (or at least emphasized) in the sign.

In the same movement, the science of the letter sets itself up in linguistics and destroys it—a paradoxical and almost untenable position. How does one found a science if one destroys its founding element? How does one destroy a science while nonetheless maintaining all its concepts? Can we even (for this is what is at issue here) refound or recast an already constituted science by challenging, in its very own terms, what constitutes it as a science? This is more than just an untenable position, it is an impossible task. The science of the letter would be just that impossible task: *a linguistics without a theory of the sign.* How could such a thing function?

In fact it does not—or not as such. It is not by chance that a kind of parentheses begins at this point in the text, which defers or suspends the demonstration in the course of a tangled and difficult page. Apparently the point is to indicate, as though for the sake of memory, the stakes, or the exact scope of the break introduced in the theory of the sign: nothing less, one might say, than the closure and condemnation of the entire *philosophical* problematic of the sign. Actually, the movement initiated here is much more complex, or if one prefers, more ambiguous.

The philosophical problematic of the sign is the question of the *arbitrary:* "This primordial distinction"—the cut of the sign—says Lacan, "goes well beyond the discussion concerning the arbitrariness of the sign, as it has been elaborated since the earliest reflections of the ancients" (*E.,* 497/149). This is a false or futile discussion, since in the closure of this question any response that one can offer "turns us away from the locus in which language questions us as to its very nature" (*E.,* 498/150).

But why precisely?

It is not in fact the arbitrariness of the sign as such which is challenged. We can even wonder if we should not say *"on the contrary."* For what is challenged is a certain way in which the question of the arbitrary has been posed, or more precisely, the treatment of language that a certain positing of the arbitrary obliges. This positing of the arbitrary is the recognition (post-Cratylian if you will) of the aporia of *reference:* "The impasse," Lacan says, "which through the same period has been encountered in every discussion of the bi-univocal correspondence between the word to the thing, if only in the mere act of naming" (*E.,* 497/149). All "evil," in other words, comes from having conceived language in relation to the thing. For if one starts with the break between the sign and the thing, it is hardly possible to go beyond the Augustinian response[4] (no "signification can be sustained other than by reference to another signification" [*E.,* 498/150]), or the nominalist or conceptualist solution ("If we try to grasp in language the constitution of the object, we cannot fail to notice that this constitution is to be found only at the level of concept, a very different thing from a simple nominative, and that the *thing,* when reduced to the noun, breaks up into the double, divergent beam of the cause in which it has taken shelter in the French word *chose,* and the nothing [*rien*] to which it has abandoned its Latin dress (*rem*) [*E.,* 498/150]).

Since the sign is arbitrary, it is hardly possible, in other words, to go beyond a recognition of a necessary link between the signifier and the signified. The entirety of linguistics, or its awkwardly philosophical double, logical neopositivism, remains caught in this very recognition, which covers, more or less explicitly, the whole field of metaphysics. This is why Lacan does not take issue directly with Saussure (whose hesitation regarding the question of the arbitrary is well known) but rather with the subsequent modifications which cannot be said to be the result of some delay of linguistics with regard to its own scientificity. For example—and this is an allusion to Benveniste's immotivation[5]—the following observation, which settles the difficulty of the arbitrariness of the signifier: "there is no language in existence for which there is any question of its inability to cover the whole field of the signified, it being an effect of its existence as a language that it necessarily answers all needs"; and also, that which in logical positivism requires the reduplication of the question of meaning, "in search of the meaning of meaning" (*E.,* 498/150), that is to say, requires the questioning of the meaning of a system of significations closed on itself.

Language is thus not to be conceived on the basis of the sign. In sum, since the emergence of the theory of the sign—that is, since that thinking which "unmotivates" the sign in order to better "motivate" the signifier in its relation to the signified—one cannot transgress the law of *representation:* a law which is illusion itself.

These considerations, important as their existence is for the philosopher, turn us away from the locus in which language questions us as to its very nature. And we will fail to pursue the question further as long as we cling to the illusion that the signifer answers to the function of representing the signified, or better, that the signifier has to answer for its existence in the name of any signification whatever. (*E.,* 498/150)

One understands better now, no doubt, in what sense it is a question of tearing linguistics away from the philosophy of the sign and of destroying the sign, in order to consolidate the science of the letter. This implies working the sign to the point of destroying its entire representational function, that is, the relation of signification itself. This is very precisely the role and the function of the algorithm. The algorithm is not the sign. Or rather: the algorithm is the sign insofar as it does not signify (in the mode of the representation of the signified by the signifier). Perhaps we could go so far as to write: the algorithm is the ~~sign~~ (under erasure). A sign under erasure, rather than a sign destroyed. A sign not functioning. None of the concepts of the theory of the sign disappear: signifier, signified, and signification are still there. But their system is disrupted, perverted.

The operation which the algorithm undergoes is precisely what brings about the perversion of the system of the sign. In fact, once the division is established in the sign (the bar accentuated), the operation essentially bears on the signifier: it subjects the signifier to such a displacement that it can no longer be taken as an element of the sign, but must rather be considered as a paradoxical concept: that of a signifier without signification.

This is why the operation consists in *differentiating* between the Saussurean schema of the sign and the schema of the algorithm. This proves, this time definitively, that the algorithm

$$\frac{S}{s}$$

is not as such comparable to the Saussurean schema. In fact, the only thing comparable to it is its *illustration.*

The Saussurean schema chosen by Lacan is the schema of the *tree.* Saussure, we know, rendered it in the following way[6]:

Lacan reproduces it by inverting it and by eliminating the ellipse as well as the two arrows of the association:

TREE

Then he replaces it with the schema of the algorithm (it is important to reproduce this schema as accurately as possible, including the handles of the doors):

MEN	WOMEN

This produces a kind of parodic double of the Saussurean schema. But exactly in what does the difference consist?

We see that, without greatly extending the scope of the signifier concerned in the experiment, that is, by dou-bling a noun through the mere juxtaposition of two terms whose complementary meanings ought apparently to reinforce each other, a surprise is produced by the unexpected precipitation of an unexpected meaning: the image of twin doors symbolizing, with the solitary confinement offered Western man for the satisfaction of his natural needs away from home, the imperative that he seems to share with the great majority of primitive communities by which his public life is subjected to the laws of urinary segregation. (*E.,* 500/151, slightly modified)

Let us analyze this passage:

1. Two terms are inscribed over the bar, in place of the signifier (or of Saussure's "acoustic image"). In the first moment of the operation, the signifier is reduplicated, or more precisely, there is an introduction of a duality, that is to say a difference, in the signifier. In the Saussurean system, this juxtaposition (which is obviously possible) would have made difference play the role of a consolidation of the *value* of each of the terms—and thus of their complementary *value*. But this schema is precisely not Saussurean. Indeed:

2. In place of the expected signified (or concept)—what should be, for example, masculine and feminine silhouettes— we find "the image of twin doors." Either the entire schema reproduces or figures an apparatus which is quite real (a public rest room or at least its facade) or, in place of the signified, another function is introduced which erases it. In a particularly ambiguous formulation (insofar as it apparently makes it impossible to differentiate between the symbolic and the real) Lacan speaks of *symbolization:* "The image of twin doors...symbolizing *with* solitary confinement...the imperative, etc." (the indecidability here is contained in this "with"). We will return in a moment to this ambiguity. Let us simply say here that, in the place of the signified, the *symbolization of a law* is introduced, which is a law of sexual segregation, and which is, as Lacan indicates, practically universal, and in this respect comparable to the general laws of culture.

3. Finally, the passage of the signifier into that symbolization (the equivalent, therefore, of the process in which signification is engendered) is presented as a "precipitation of meaning." This is a remarkable formulation, since it lends itself to at least three interpretations, which are, moreover, amusing: for this can just as well mean that meaning falls head first (and one does not say where...), or that meaning goes too fast, that it short-circuits the signified (man and woman, as concepts, are hardly audible any longer but through the door), or finally, that meaning precipitates in the chemical sense of the word, that is to say that it settles as such amidst the solution of the signifier.

We see consequently that the "silencing" of the nominalist debate (with a low blow) consists in purely and simply suppressing the entire question of reference (understood as determining the position of the signified) in order to replace it with an "access" of the signifier to the signified (*E.,* 501/152), an "entry" of the signifier into the signified (*E.,* 500/151) through, or rather by, the play of the signifier alone, which is here confirmed in its threefold determination: materiality/localization/symbolization.

What must now be reconstituted is this process of "signification," or at least its first moment, if the algorithmic schema is to later prove unable, by itself, to entirely ensure the production of "meaning."

What founds the process described here in its entirety is, as we just saw, the law of urinary segregation, or the law as law of *the difference of sexes.* Or, to remain faithful to the terminology of the text, we could say the *imperative.* This imperative determines, in turn, a material separation that the signifier comes to inscribe as distinct places (the twofold solitary confinement—and here we presumably ought to take the expression *solitary confinement* in the strongest sense of the term). The signifier is thus the difference of places, the very possibility of localization. This explains its "odd" materiality, as was said, we remember, in the "Seminar on 'The Purloined

Letter.'" It does not divide itself into places, it divides places—that is to say, it institutes them. This amounts to saying, if you will, that there is not a division because there is materiality, but rather that there is materiality because there is division. Moreover, the linguistic signifier *Men/Women* does not inscribe itself on these places to bring about a direct referral to the signified (the "concepts" of men and women), but only inscribes itself as difference. Namely, *Men≠Women,* which is to say, the law itself.

This can be considered, in fact, as being symbolic in two ways:

1. In the sense of symbolic or algorithmic logic, to the extent that we are only dealing here with *differential marks* (the relation of which the theory of symbolic logic itself compares to the relation of places in a topology). Hence the example of the short-sighted person on this same page 500/151: "for the blinking gaze of the short-sighted person might be justified in wondering whether this was indeed the signifier as he peered closely at the little enamel signs that bore it, a signifier whose signified would in this case receive its final honors from the double and solemn procession from the upper nave." The short-sighted person thus deciphers neither the signification of the facade of the rest room, nor the signified of the inscribed signifier (Men, Women), but rather the difference as such between the places. This may be schematized roughly in the following way:

$$(M) \longleftarrow \neq \longrightarrow (W)$$

It can also be understood as the place assigned to one, for example, as man. Under the bar, therefore, one finds man's solitary confinement and not the signified (man), to which one would otherwise have to attribute the very function of solitary confinement: namely, of receiving the "final honors" of men and women whom the signifier separates into a parallel procession. Such a *Witz* is, obviously, only possible, we may note, if one plays on the ambiguity of the schema, which can be either realistic or symbolic—an ambiguity which is itself carefully woven into the entire text, and particularly into the proposition we cited earlier: "the image of twin doors symbolizing...with the solitary confinement...the imperative, etc." This passage can thus be read in the following way:

—Either: the image of twin doors which, along with the solitary confinement, symbolize the imperative...

—Or: the image of twin doors which symbolize both the solitary confinement and the imperative.

2. It may also be considered in the classical sense of the word, insofar as the *symbol* is not entirely unmotivated, but always retains something of the reality to which it refers (for instance, the "natural link" Saussure speaks about). In other words, here the set Men/Women does not have the law as its signified, but rather symbolizes the difference articulated by the law through the spacing which constitutes the signified as such.

With respect to this entire operation we could propose the following rough schema:

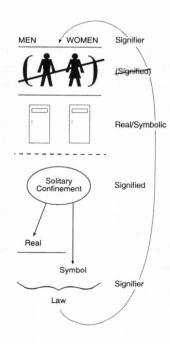

Given that is is correct, this schema is only worth whatever schemas of its kind are usually worth. But it does not measure up, in any case, to the illustration which Lacan himself proposes, since "no contrived example can be as telling as the actual experience of truth" (*E.*, 500/151). And in fact:

> A train arrives at a station. A little boy and a little girl, brother and sister, are seated in a compartment face to face next to a window through which the buildings along the station platform can be seen passing as the train pulls to a stop. "Look," says the brother, "we're at Ladies!" "Idiot!" replies his sister, "Can't you see we're at Gentlemen."
>
> Besides the fact that the rails in this story materialize the bar in the Saussurean algorithm (and in a form designed to symbolize that its resistance may be other than dialectical), we should add that only someone who didn't have his eyes in front of the holes (it's the appropriate image here) could possibly confuse the place of the signifier and the signified in this story, or not see from what radiating centre the signifier sends forth its light into the shadow of incomplete significations. (*E.*, 500/152)

Because they occupy distinct and opposed places, the two children choose the inscription which corresponds to the place of each as a name for the stop (without deciphering therefore, the signified). Each inscription (or each place) is the exclusion of the other. Each time, then, the choice made happens to be that of the opposite sex. Lacan immediately relates this to castration (the hole, the radiating center) and reads it as its inscription (on the condition, however, that one consider castration itself as ultimately related, as we will see, to the signifying hole [the hole of the signifier]). In other words, a purely signifying, purely toponymical usage corresponds to a positing of sexual difference on the basis of what determines such difference—the presence/absence of the penis (but in this case, on the condition that one refer this alternative to the structural alternative, where, as it is said in the "Seminar on 'The Purloined Letter,'" "presence/absence take their cue from each other" [*E.,* 46.]). Consequently, it is only from this "center" that one can reach the signified, the latter, moreover, found only in darkness and incompletion. The children remain symbolically separated from signification by the rails, or, if one prefers, the rails (not being "dialectical") prevent signification. Moreover, the commentary which immediately follows clearly indicates that natural, animal sexual difference is not the difference in question, and that only the usage of the signifier is able to inscribe it as such, raising it to the level of the Dissension (the mytheme of primordial Ερις) on the basis of which the boundless war of tragedy or the irreducible duality of the Platonic countries is engendered.

We understand better now what the signifier means to Lacan—or rather to what displacement Lacan subjects it ("I have defined the signifier as no one has dared").[7] It is no longer the other side of the sign in relation to the signified, and consisting only in this association, but rather it is that order of spacing, according to which the law is inscribed and marked as difference. It is even the *structural hole,* as the signifier should now be referred to, according to which the law is marked as difference.

All the same, the operation itself remains to be produced. It is necessary to ensure the functioning of the algorithm, that is, to allow the signifier alone to support the entire weight of this functioning, since "signification" cannot go through the signified. This provides an "entry" into the signified, but without relying at any time on any signified. In the terms of the railway illustration—the ambiguity of the symbolic, let us note in passing, continues there—the signifier must cross the rails and reach the children (through the door, the corridor, or the plumbing of the train).

The "formula" of this operation is the following:

Insofar as it is itself only pure function of the signifier, the algorithm can only reveal the structure of a signifier in this transfer. (*E.,* 501/152.)

This formula, as we can see, is neither clear nor univocal, for what is binding here, what commands the entire process is the fact that the algorithm itself is a "pure function of the signifier." Now this may be understood in two ways:

—Either *function of the signifier* means, quite simply, that the algorithm is written in terms of the signifier, or, more precisely, that it is the notation of the position and process of the signifier. This amounts to saying that the algorithm takes its value from its content as it has been determined, but insofar as, given this formulation, the predominance of the signifier is accentuated (by the *purity* of the function). If the algorithm is to be read as the notation of the signifier alone, and of an operation for which it suffices—if the algorithm is only written to indicate the self-sufficient primacy of the signifier—the signified which appears there (or rather what takes its place) is only there for memory's sake or as a secondary effect, which is derived from the signifying operation with which it is in no way contemporaneous, and in which it does not even participate. But we already know that it is impossible to read the algorithm in this way.

—Or the formula *pure function of the signifier* indicates that the signifier functions *as* an algorithm, that is to say, according to the algorithmic nature of the algorithm. Indeed, according to the expression on page 498/150, the algorithm has *no meaning*. This absence of meaning is due to the autonomous functioning of the algorithmic chain insofar as it is conceived as a chain of differential marks which mark nothing by themselves except their reciprocal positions and the relations (or combinations) through which a "meaning" is fabricated (a meaning which is itself not defined by the aim of any content, or signified, whether empirical or true).

This is evidently what is in question here. But the concept of *mark* still retains something too positive in it. This is in fact why Lacan substitutes another "model" for it, that of an algorithm as "hole," whose differential logic (a *purely* differential one, if that means anything) determines the entire order of the signifier. It is moreover necessary to have recourse here to another of Lacan's texts, "Subversion of the Subject and the Dialectic of Desire" (a later text, from 1960, but which was written, as Lacan indicates, on the basis of a seminar contemporary with the "Agency of the Letter"), from which we will borrow two formulas which may shed light on the play of what we must henceforth call *the logic of the signifier.*

> The signifier is constituted only from a synchronic and enumerable collection of elements in which each is sustained only by the principle of its opposition to each of the others. (*E.,* 806/304)
>
> If linguistics enables us to see the signifier as the determinant of the signified, analysis reveals the truth of this relation by making the "holes" in meaning the determinants of its discourse. (*E.,* 801/299)

We must however add the following: a final determination, on the basis of which the play organizes itself in its entirety, is grafted onto this determination of the play of the signifier, as a relation of the holes of meaning. It is a signifier that Lacan names *"the signifier of a lack in the Other."* If the Other, as we already know, is indeed the guarantor, that is to say, the condition of the possibility of speech, this is because it is, primordially, something like the originary signifier from which the signifying combination is woven. But this is on the condition that the originary signifier be nothing by itself—and nothing to the point of not admitting an Other (which would be the Other of the Other—God, if you will, or a zero symbol). On the contrary, it is the signifier of the very *lack* of such a symbol (and of God?), on the basis of which the chain of signifiers can be articulated. This is the signifier "without which all the others would represent nothing," the pure gap of the signifier in general. Hence the necessity of this third reference:

> And since the battery of signifiers, as such, is by that very fact complete, this signifier can only be a line [*trait*] that is drawn from its circle without being able to be counted part of it. It can be symbolized by the inherence of a (-1) in the whole set of signifiers.
>
> As such it is inexpressible, but its operation is not inexpressible. (*E.*, 819/316)

There is therefore something like a pure *operativity* at the basis of what Lacan himself will later name *signifiance*— though this operative (or mechanical) sense is not explicitly thematized as the moment of the destruction of meaning, still less as the opposition of meaning and operation. We will return to this. For the moment, it suffices to note that it is on the basis of this pure operativity that the operation draws its possibility and that the logic of the signifier is founded, that is to say both its autonomy and its functioning which is paradoxically "centered" on a hole or a lack.

In that case, it may finally seem possible to ensure entry into the signified, which has been anticipated for some time. But this is not the case. It has not occurred yet. It must still be shown that meaning can in fact be produced from the letter alone. It must still be shown to what extent one can do without the sign. This is the object of what we will determine, consequently, as the third part of this text, and to which we have given the following title, which in a few pages will no longer be surprising: "The Tree of the Signifier."

Notes

1. Ferdinand de Saussure, *Course in General Linguistics,* trans., Wade Baskin (New York: McGraw Hill, 1966), p. 114.

2. Roland Barthes, *Elements of Semiology,* trans., Annette Lavers and Colin Smith (New York: Hill & Wang, 1968), p. 49.

3.

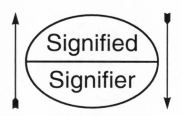

4. Lacan refers here to Augustine's *The Teacher,* in *The Teacher; The Free Choice of the Will; Grace and Free Will,* trans., Robert Russell (Washington: Catholic University of America Press, 1968).

5. Cf. Emile Benveniste, "The Nature of the Linguistic Sign" (1939) in *Problems in General Linguistics,* p. 43.

6. Saussure, *Course in General Linguistics,* p. 67.

7. "Radiophonie," Scilicet no. 2/3, p. 65.

The Tree of the Signifier

The formula on which we have just commented ("for the algorithm, being itself but a pure function of the signifier can only reveal a structure of signifier to this transference") thus designates the constraint or the properly *structural* conditions of the signifying operation. It is that structure-like nature of the signifier that Lacan posits as *articulation:* "But the structure of the signifier is, as is commonly said of language, to be articulated" (*E.,* 501/152).

This means two things:

1. From the perspective of their "increasing inclusions" (which is to say, in Saussurean language, from the perspective of the system), the signifying unities break up into "ultimate differential elements" (*E.,* 501/152) which are the phonemes of phonology, the essential "differential coupling" of which Lacan particularly emphasizes.

This is why, as we can now understand, a certain privilege is granted to the φωνή that predestines it for alphabetical writing. Hence the use of the word *letter,* which here gathers together the essential features of the signifier in the form of typographical characters: its materiality and its ability to be localized on the one hand, and its differential structure on the other.

> Through this one sees that an essential element of the spoken word itself was predestined to flow into the mobile characters which, in a jumble of lower case Didots or Garamonds, render validly present what we

call the "letter," namely, the essentially localized structure of the signifier. (*E.*, 501/153)

This decomposition defines, in general, the order of the *lexicon*, which is to say, "the order of the constitutive inclusions of
the signifier," whose upper limit is the "verbal phrase" (*E.*,
502/153).

2. From the perspective of their "reciprocal trespassing"
(in Saussurean terms, the syntagm), these same signifying unities join together "according to the laws of a closed order" (*E.*,
501/ 153). Lacan defines that order as a *topology*, which is to
say, a pure combination of places of which an "approximation"
can be given by the figure of the *signifying chain* borrowed
from Hjelmslev[1]: "rings of a necklace," Lacan says, "which is a
ring in another necklace made of rings" (*E.*, 502/153). This is, in
general, the grammar whose limit is the unit immediately supe-
rior to the sentence.

The signifying articulation can thus be described according
to the two Saussurean axes of syntagm and system, but only
on the condition of maintaining the operation of the pure signifying structure beyond the point where, from a strictly linguistic perspective, the conditions of possibility provided by
the structure give way to the production of meaning.

Thus in the horizontal or linear dimension of speech, Lacan
does not emphasize the completion or achievement of meaning
(since "none of the elements of the chain *consist* in the signification of which it is at the moment capable" [*E.*, 502/153]), but
rather the signifier's incessant anticipation of meaning. Hence
the use of unfinished sentences: "It remains that..., Never do
I..., Still perhaps..." which produce a signifying effect precisely
where they cease to posit signs and thus suspend meaning. This
use refers, for instance, to the analysis of the Schreber case that
Lacan had developed two years earlier and took up again in the
text entitled, "On a Question Preliminary to any Possible
Treatment of Psychosis" (*E.*, 539–40/185–87).

Lacan nevertheless relates this anticipation to the Saussurean theory of the "two floating kingdoms." But one suspects that he does so in order to distort it, given what he needs to get out of it. We know that for Saussure[2] the issue is to describe the formation of the sign as the *simultaneous* division of two float-ing masses, that of sounds and that of thoughts, within which neither sounds nor concepts appear as such *before* the division of language. Hence the well-known schema:

(confused ideas)

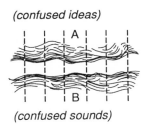

(confused sounds)

Lacan says that this schema illustrates "the incessant slid-ing of the signified under the signifier." But this manner of putting the sign back on its feet, if we may use an expression which is famous in another context and not unexpected here, does not simply mean the *reversal* of the schema to which we are now accustomed. To speak of the sliding of one of the terms instead of the floating of the two obviously means more than just distorting or reversing—not only because, once again, the signified is the victim, but because the Saussurean "image" invoked here does not, for good reasons, lend itself to this type of treatment. Furthermore, this is why Lacan ostensibly takes it as a mere image, in order to expose its fragility: "an image resembling the wavy lines of the upper and lower waters in miniatures from manuscripts of *Genesis;* a double flux marked by fine streaks of rain, vertical dotted lines supposedly confin-ing segments of correspondence" (*E.,* 502–3/154).

This is indeed a critique ("All our experience runs counter..."). One must maintain the independence and preex-istence of the signifier against the Saussurean schema of the sign which subordinates the constitution of the signifier and the signified to the preliminary division of the sign and which

posits the co-extension of the chain of signifieds with the signifying chain. Hence the endless sliding of the signified. But it
seems, curiously, that one runs into a difficulty, which had up to
now been carefully put aside or deferred. If indeed the signified constantly evades the grasp of the signifier, if the *signifier*
never *consists* in such or such punctual *signification,* if nothing
stops the movement or the mobility of a meaning always torn
from itself, expelled from itself, how can one give an account at
least of the *effect* of signification or meaning? By defering the
very movement which is to be thought, by defering, thus, the
position of this question, or more precisely the treatment of
this question, the operation of perversion (or as Lacan says, of
the *diversion* of the Saussurean system) would be made possible (at least up to a certain point). And we will see, in a
moment, that once the fault discovered here has been precipi-
tously (and allusively) closed again, the operation of diversion
will persist for a time. But the schema of the "floating kingdoms" resists. The schema of the "floating kingdoms" no
longer merely gives an account of the sign in general but rather
of the concrete functioning of language itself, which necessi-
tates, as we know, moving from *signification* to *value.*[3]

We know that the "solution" is the so-called theory of
"anchoring points" [*points de capiton*]—which is (in *The Agency*) simply named or invoked. This theory claims that in order
for a signification to be produced at a given time, it is necessary
that the signifier interrupt the sliding of the signified at certain
places by something like an anchoring phenomenon which
gives rise to *punctuation* "where the signification is constituted
as a finished product."[4] This is the case whether we see
between pages 805/303 and 808/306 of *Ecrits* the construction
of the *graph* of the "anchoring point," or whether we quite simply substitute a cross-section of a bed, as it were, for the "river"
of the Saussurean schema of the "floating kingdoms."

Of course one must recall that the anchoring point is presented by Lacan as *mythical:* there is no signification which is
not always already sliding outside of its alleged proper mean-

ing. This is emphasized, for example, in the text of a seminar given on January 22, 1958, and cited by Laplanche in the Bonneval symposium on the unconscious:

> Between the two chains...that of the signifiers in relation to the circulation of travelling signifieds which are always in the process of sliding, the pinning-down or anchoring point I am speaking about or even the anchoring point is mythical, for no one has ever been able to pin a signification onto a signifier; but on the other hand one can pin a signifier onto a signifier and see what happens. But in this case something new always occurs...namely, the emergence of a new signification...[5]

The difficulty has indeed been put aside, at least provisionally. It has nevertheless disrupted the discursive linearity of the demonstration, in the course of a paragraph, as if by accident. Now it is precisely and paradoxically the Saussurean linearity itself which disturbs this whole discourse. Indeed, if one considers this passage as an oblique "commentary" on Chapter Four of *The Course,* it is not unimportant to note at this point (even if we have to return to it later) that it is nonetheless linearity which constitutes the principle of language as a system of differences "without positive terms"— this is why it offers this "term of comparison" which is the material writing of the letters.[6] Lacan says, "the linearity that Saussure holds to be constitutive of the chain of discourse, in conformity with its emission by a single voice and with its horizontal position in our writing—if this linearity is indeed necessary, it is not sufficient" (*E.,* 503/154). One would almost be led, then, to reject linearity. Certainly, the bypassing of something like Saussure's "positivism" remains at issue here. As soon as it is a question of the sign as such (and no longer only of the signified and the signifier "taken separately")—specifically as soon as the fourth paragraph of Chapter Four—this positivism modifies the theory of pure differences (*"in lan-*

guage there are only differences") in favor of a doctrine of combination conceived of as a "positive fact," and further-more, "the only kind of facts that language contains": "When we compare signs—positive terms—with each other, we can no longer speak of difference."[7] But is this sufficient to account for the fact that the only necessity granted to linearity is defined by the temporal orientation it imposes on dis-course—a recognition which would rather seem, in fact, to save linearity *in extremis* by allowing it "to be taken as a signi-fying factor," at least in the languages where the grammatical distinction of the object and the subject allows an inversion of time to take place, as in the inversion of the terms of such a proposition as "Paul hits Pierre" instead of "Pierre hits Paul," since, as we all know, it all depends on "who started it"?

In fact—and we will no doubt have to return to this *coup de force*—if linearity is not *sufficient,* it is because it *"suffices* [our emphasis] to listen to poetry...for a polyphony to be heard, for it to become clear that all discourse is aligned along the several staves of a score" (*E.,* 503/154). What then *essen-tially* constitutes discourse is not the syntagmatic articulation, the syntactical horizontality of the chain, but the paradigmatic or systematic depth, the play of semantic or lexical correla-tions. Linearity is as problematical as verticality (the promised land...) is self-evident. And it is no accident if it is introduced here by a metaphor (the analogy of music) which is perhaps the metaphor of metaphoricity in general. Clearly, the conse-quences of this *turn* will be considerable, and we will have to measure its effects progressively. But first it must be analyzed: what in fact is taking place?

What is taking place is quite simply that the difficulty related to linearity that required "anchoring" and punctua-tion, against all expectation (that is to say, in spite of the stat-ed intention to continue to defer the crossing of the bar and the entry into the signified in order to ensure the possibility of a pure *significance*), this difficulty itself authorizes and grounds the *poetic* aim of language.

There is in effect no signifying chain that does not have, as if attached to the *punctuation* of each of its units, a whole articulation of relevant contexts suspended "vertically," as it were, from that *point.* (*E.,* 503/154, our emphasis)

Moreover, this is what immediately makes it possible to resume the *diversion* of Saussure, a treatment that can only be defined by its *witzig* character (in the most romantic sense of the word). The graphic *Witz* of the schema is replaced by another, this time verbal, and grounded on an anagram [*barre*] of the Saussurean *tree* [*arbre*].[8]

Let us take our word "tree" again, this time not as an isolated noun, but at the point of one of these punctuations, and we will see that it is not because the word *barre* is the anagram of *arbre,* that the latter crosses the bar of the Saussurean algorithm. (*E.,* 503/154, translation modified)

This is a purely restrictive precaution. For with respect to this tree, a sort of demonstration of the power of poetry, itself poetic, follows immediately—or, as they say in literature manuals, of the *evocative* power of the word. This reference is not inappropriate, insofar as this whole exercise ultimately rests on what has been called, in the wake of symbolism (and we know how far it spreads), the *alchemy of the Word* or the *evocatory sorcery.* It is thus not a question of *commenting on* this text (but still, the reader might consult Littré on the word *tree*). It is no doubt preferable to quite simply offer it (again) to be read, that is (more than ever in this exposé), to be *heard.*

For even broken down into the double spectre of its vowels and consonants, it can still call up with the robur and the plane tree the signification it takes on, in the context of our flora, of strength and majesty. Drawing on all the symbolic contexts suggested in the Hebrew of the Bible, it erects on a barren hill the shadow of a

cross. Then reduces to the capital Y, the sign of dichoto-
my which, except for the illustration used by heraldry,
would owe nothing to the tree however genealogical we
may think it. Circulatory tree, tree of life of the cerebel-
lum, tree of Saturn, tree of Diana, crystals formed in a
tree struck by lightning, is it your figure that traces our
destiny for us in the tortoise shell cracked by the fire, or
your lightning that causes that slow shift in the axis of
being to surge up from an unamable night into the Εν
Πάντα of language:

> *No! says the Tree, it says No! in the shower of sparks*
> *Of its superb head*

lines that require the harmonics of the tree just as
much as their continuation:

> *Which the storm treats as universally*
> *As it does a blade of grass.*

For this modern verse is ordered according to the
same law of the parallelism of the signifier that creates
the harmony governing the primitive Slavic epic or the
most refined Chinese poetry.

As is seen in the fact that the tree and the blade of
grass are chosen from the same mode of the existent in
order for the signs of contradiction—saying "No!" and
"treat as"—to affect them, and also so as to bring
about, through the categorical contrast of the particu-
larity of *superb* with the *universally* that reduces it, in
the condensation of the "head" [*tête*] and the "storm"
[*tempête*] the indiscernible shower of sparks of the eter-
nal instant. (*E.*, 504/154–55)

Hence, in this way, or in this style, the crossing of the bar,
that is, the production of meaning, actually occurs before
being treated as such in the exposé. A meaning that will have
been given prior to the utterance of its own possibility, since,

from the perspective of the demonstration, everything remains to be said.

This is why, once the verse of the tree is completed, once the turn is achieved, we must still labor to reveal the signifying operation. Hence the following section that we are finally able to entitle, "Signifiance."

Notes

1. Louis Hjelmslev, *Language: An Introduction,* trans., Francis J. Whitfield (Madison: University of Wisconsin Press, 1970), p. 32.

2. *Course in General Linguistics,* p.111–12.

3. Ibid., p. 113–14.

4. "Subversion of the Subject…," *E.,* 806/304.

5. In Laplanche-Leclaire, "l'Inconscient, une étude psychanalytique," *l'Inconscient: VIe Colloque de Bonneval,* 1960 (Paris: Desclée de Brouwer, 1966) p. 118, translation ours.

6. Saussure, p. 118–19.

7. Ibid., p. 121.

8. We can hardly avoid noting, in passing, that another sort of anagram (where another unconscious is in question) was put into play by Saussure himself, and that we could interrogate this enterprise in order to know to what extent it might have been another diversion of or another *Witz* played on linguistics. This would add a supplementary and peculiar complexity to the relations of Saussure and Lacan, which begin to become entangled here.

4.

Signifiance

The articulated apparatus of the letter has thus been described and put in place, as it confers its structure on the signifier, or even as it structurally constitutes the signifier. For the moment, we can neglect the poetic twist [*tour*] by which this signifier just crossed the bar, since it will not be long before the same twist will insist anew.

Perhaps one sees better now how the description of articulation has been divided, all along, between two levels corresponding to a double meaning of the term "signifier."

On the one hand, in effect, the signifier is conveived as *algorithm,* that is to say, as a self-sufficient unit, which, once posited, develops its properties autocratically in a combinatory and "localized" mode (*E.,* 501/153).

On the other hand, it is conceived, however obliquely, as the signifying *operation* for which the algorithm must ultimately function. The signifying operation is the paradoxical maintaining, under the signifier "signifier," of at least a part of its linguistic concept, that is, of the Saussurean concept of the "acoustic image" (which is, in a secondary sense, graphic) insofar as it is part of the sign and thus insofar as it is an element of (and in) signification. It is a question thus of this active, productive sense implied in the present participle on the basis of which the word *signifiant*[1] is formed, and it is this sense which will determine, in the final analysis (at the end of algorithmic calculus) what Lacan will call a bit further on "*signifiance*" (E. 510/159).

This operation must be more *properly* questioned. Yet, as

we shall soon see, it is precisely the property [*la propriété*] or propriety [*le propre*][2] of such an operation—of what Lacan himself calls "the properly signifying function" (*E.,* 505/156)—which will be put into question in its very establishment. *Signifiance,* indeed, is the operation of the signifier when it has "passed over to the level of the signified," as Lacan says, and when it comes thus "to be charged with signification" (*E.,* 504/155).

If *signifiance* is thus absolutely, rigorously and simply not signification itself, it is nonetheless that which makes signification possible, and even that which tends, of itself, to constitute it. When the term *signifiance* appears in *The Agency* (*E.,* 510/159), it is in order to translate the *Deutung* of Freud's *Traumdeutung.* In German, the prefix *be-* is needed to form *Bedeutung,* or *signification* (the prefix serving to mark the act or the operation of *giving* meaning, of *rendering* significant in the ordinary sense of the word). In French, an ending is needed to go from "*signifiance*" to "signification." *Signifiance* operates thus at *the edge* of signification, that is to say that it touches on what until now has been excluded from the signifying order by Lacan.

But this is also why the treatment of *signifiance* will reinvest, on the very edge of signification, the entire autonomous and autocratic value of the signifier (namely, in the final analysis, all the resistant value of the *bar*)—a value which we could name, in all rigor, *nonsignifying.*

In accordance with the literality of the signifier, the production of meaning must occur without the signified being taken into account. It is thus necessary to understand, in the formula that opens this part of the text (*E.,* 504/155), that "to pass over to the level of the signified" is always, and perhaps can only be: to pass *to the limit* of the signified, in other words, without crossing that limit (or having already exceeded it, but precisely in such a way that the signified is immediately exhausted, punctuation dissolved and sliding perpetuated).

One should consequently maintain these two theses simultaneously—certainly not an easy task: *signifiance* crosses the bar, and *signifiance* only slides along the bar.

The composition of the text in this passage already testifies to this antinomial operation (*E.,* 504–9/155–59). In effect, the operation of the signifier is first announced by the introduction of the *subject* into the problematic. "But this whole signifier can only operate, it will be said, if it is present in the subject" (*E.,* 504/155, slightly modified). In fact, barely half a page will be devoted to this "subject." It suffices for Lacan to have granted that meaning can only take place by and for the subject—a determination which is not only "classical" but absolutely inherent in the terms that compose it—for him immediately to assign the whole production of meaning to a tropological play [*tropique*], that of metaphor and metonymy, where subjectivity no longer intervenes, and which occupies the rest of the passage, forming by the same token the conclusion of this first part of Lacan's essay.

The trick [*tour*] thus played on the subject can only be understood in terms of the treatment to which it is here submitted. We must begin to dwell, then, on this treatment, even if this means giving the commentary inverse proportions to those of the text.

Signification, understood as the "presence" of the signifier "in the subject," is in fact what was implied earlier in the idea of an access to the signified or of an entry of the signifier into the signified—the exhibition of which was necessarily deferred.

That the subject is the locus of signification is sufficiently indicated by the definition of the *sign* that Lacan gives most often: "The sign is what represents something for someone."[3] By "something," the definition emphasizes what we have already noted and must recall: namely, that Lacan, while borrowing the elements of his thematic (signifier, signified, etc.) from the linguistic (Saussurean) sign, sets aside the function in which, and for which, these elements as such are brought together in linguistics—that is, he sets aside the function of *sign,* or the function of signification as a representational function (and in the final analysis, as a referential function). It is for the same reason that elsewhere he is able to reserve the name "sign"—according to the definition just recalled—for the pure indexical function of what he calls, for example, the "sign language" of animals.[4] Lacan's "sign" thus includes the concept of the sign as *reference.* Indeed, because of his discrete but tenacious insistence on the motif of an almost direct, immediate referentiality (we recall the exclusion of the "thing" and its corollary, the will to escape the entire philosophical tradition of the sign; we will see this motif function later in the constitution of tropes), he goes so far as to identify the sign with a simple *signal,* or simple *index,* in the Peircean sense. The sign here is pure reference, that is to say, that against which the resistance of the bar was posited, with the autonomy of the signifier.

The latter, on the contrary, fulfills the function of *signifiance,* in which there could not be any presentation or indication of the referent, of the "something." But by abandoning the "something," the signifier also necessarily abandons its correlate, the "someone." In *signifiance,* if there is no referent, neither can there be the one for whom there can be (or should be) reference in general—or more exactly there cannot be that which, in relation to referentiality, takes on by the same token the form and the status of a "someone," of a subject.

Thus, on the page just cited, Lacan extends his definition of the sign with the following addition: "but the status of this someone is uncertain."

It is this "uncertainty" of the subject that we must consequently consider, at the very point where the subject turns up in our text. We will be concerned with a two-fold determination:

1. On the one hand, the subject of signification, at least of this "signification" whose "words" are ready "to be charged"[5] in the purely signifying operation (*E.,* 504/155), is not subjectivity in the sense of being a master of meaning. Signification is no more able to come to an end or a stop than the signified is able to escape from its perpetual sliding—than the subject is able to

be that which or the one who would give meaning to meaning, or make or constitute meaning. The "presence" of the signifier "in the subject" thus cannot mean, as Lacan suggests, a simple reversal of roles, the subordination of the signifier to the subject. Rather, the subject is itself commanded by that which appears within it. And the Lacanian "meaning" of the signifier "subject" is rather that of the topological [*topique*] and, as we will see, tropological [*tropique*] locus of the signifier, which amounts to the dissolution of this "meaning," its slippage into the signifying function itself.

2. On the other hand, it is necessary to state the reciprocal of this first proposition: the locus of the Lacanian signifier is nevertheless the subject. Fundamentally, and in spite of the brevity of the remarks in this passage, it is in a *theory of the subject* that the logic of the signifier settles.

To go back to this we need to start again from the text. What is surprising in the four paragraphs devoted to the subject (*E.,* 504–5/155–56) is that the process of signification is described as exceeding [*passant*] the subject and taking place [*se passant*] outside of it. Indeed, a function which was originally introduced as internal to the subject will be determined in the "something quite other" and in the "between-the-lines" (*E.,* 505/156).

Presumably the text ties this function to the aims and capacities of a subject—of that subject that "I" am, "insofar as I have this language in common with other subjects" (*E.,* 505/156). It is indeed this "I" which is here the subject of all actions, that is to say of the signifying operations: "I" can "signify" and "be understood" [*être entendu*]. But it is necessary to state immediately that this subject is not the Lacanian subject.

In order to give an account of this paradox we must consider the two levels on which the text in fact operates simultaneously, and which must be analyzed:

1. On one level, the text carries out a sort of staging of a subject in the traditional sense of the term (which is connoted,

furthermore, in an existential mode, since it behaves as a character): that is, a subject capable of signification, or of *meaning* [*vouloir-dire*] (here present in the form of "wanting to be understood" [*vouloir être entendu*] [*E.*, 505/156]).

From the traditional point of view, meaning measures itself against its contrary, nonmeaning [*le ne-pas-vouloir-dire*] (namely, in our text, the terms "to hide" [*E.*, 504/155] or "to disguise" [*E.*, 505/155]), that is to say that it always fundamentally measures itself against the aim of a truth as proper meaning or as adequation of meaning to a property.

But it is not this aim as such that holds Lacan's interest. At least, it only interests him to the extent that, within the motif of the aim of adequation, it is possible, as it were, to isolate the aim from reference (that is to say to the "thing" in regard to which the aim is able to be adequate, appropriate or inappropriate) and to work or bring the aim into play for itself. Recalling the anecdote of the two children, Lacan specifies that it would remain true even if they had no possible access to the signified—if we assume that Men/Women was written in an unknown language. The "quarrel over words," would be "no less ready," he writes, "to be charged with signification" (*E.*, 504/155).[6] (Let us add, in passing, that the children's status as "subjects" will henceforth appear problematic, and in any case displaced.) It is thus from the play of signifiers alone that signification itself can—or should?—be expected. The aim of the signified, as such, is not retained. What is retained is, if you will, the function of adequation itself, abstracted from its context, or rather detached from any adequation or appropriation to anything else than its own play. This play, in its autonomous functioning, makes a gap or alteration possible through the combination of signifiers. "To the extent that I have this language in common with other subjects"—that is on the basis of the contract and the guarantee discussed earlier—the subject of meaning is able to use this language, "in order to signify *something quite other* than what it says" (*E.*, 505/155).

The "*something quite other*" thus comes to characterize

the signifying function, or qualify its property, if one may still refer to it in that way, in place of the "something" which used to determine the function of the sign.

This can be seen, for example (but we know now that it is more than just an example), in a new exercise on the inexhaustable possibilities of the signifier "tree" [*arbre*]. To say, "*grimper à l'arbre*"[7] instead of "to be fooled," or to say "*arborer*" instead of "to wear," is to produce, not only "what the facts *communicate*" (and communication concerns or constitutes the traditional subject), but also a supplementary effect of derision, in spite of what the facts communicate. It is thus "to make truth understood *between the lines* through the signifier alone" (*E.,* 505/155, slightly modified).

It is necessary here to point out that these "acrobatics," as Lacan refers to them, amount to defining or at least describing *connotation*—namely that of which *rhetoric* is the signifier (in the linguistic sense).[8] The rest of the text will develop in this register: *signifiance* will function as a regulated generalization of connotation and by the same token will upset signification and the function of the subject.

However, that which retains this power of connotation within meaning (from which it could not escape in traditional theory, and of which it may be seen as a particularly emphatic mode) or—what amounts to the same thing—what only makes it a corollary of the power of denotation (of adequation) is that staging of a subject who is able "to know the truth": I am able indeed, "if I know the truth, to make it heard in spite of all the *between-the-lines* censures" (*E.,* 505/155).

"Knowing the truth" is what the Lacanian subject is incapable of. And it is precisely this subject deprived of knowledge who can be the subject of a connotation which is *purely and simply detached or demarcated from denotation* (since, as we see, *signifiance* can be rendered by such a formula).

2. At this point, we must move to the second level of the text, this time an implicit one—a passage which requires us to make reference to other texts in *Ecrits.*

If a subject is at issue for the theory of the letter, this subject must necessarily have been masked by what should be designated rather as the character [*personnage*] of meaning. This subject is the subject for which the sole truth, instead of being the truth of a signification or a successful adequation, is pronounced in the well-known prosopopeia (in 1956, namely, the year preceding *The Agency*)[9]: "I, the truth, I speak."

This truth—the theory of which commands, in turn, the theory of the subject—cannot be *known* by the subject. It is anterior or exterior to all knowing, since we must understand it as Lacan has since specified:[10] as the identification of truth with speech itself, without any other reference, and in particular to the exclusion of any metalanguage, that is to say of any meaning of meaning.

This truth, which "is founded by the fact that it speaks" (*E.,* 868) thus depends solely on speech, and on no other *thing* that might be designated. It only holds itself in the spacing of the signifying structure—or in the hole.

It is this very hole which is assigned to the subject by the text: when the function of "signifying *something quite other*" is presented as a function which does not aim at "disguising the thought of the subject (which is most often indefinable)" but at "indicating the place of this subject in the search for the true" (*E.,* 505/155). One cannot "disguise" what does not let itself be defined—that is to say, the subject has no property and even less an interiority that it could mask. In this sense the Lacanian truth decisively breaks with truth as adequation. The function of "signifying *something quite other*" only obeys the model of "the disguise" *in order "to disguise" "nothing,"* an absence, according to a process of the "quite other," which is that of an alterity and an alteration repeated indefinitely along the signifying chain. The "quite other" is speech itself, that is, truth. (In this sense we see that truth only deviates from the model of adequation by perverting or diverting it. This could be formulated in the following way: if it is no longer a question of the letter being adequate to something—

and in particular to an intention [*un esprit*]—it *is* a question of the adequation (truth) of the letter to a permanent and radical gesture of in-adequation.)

The subject would not be able "to signify" this "quite other" without itself becoming altered and alienated when taking its place in the sole signifying structure.

We will limit ourselves to locating this place briefly—this other localization of the hole—with a few broad strokes, by borrowing only what is absolutely necessary from outside *The Agency*.

The subject is defined as "what the signifier represents,"[11] which should be understood in the following way: if the subject is the possibility of speech, and if this speech is actualized as a signifying chain, then the relation of a signifier to another signifier, or that which a signifier "represents," as Lacan says, for another signifier—namely, the very structure of the chain—is what must be named "subject."

Hence these two definitions which compose the circle where the logic of the signifier and the theory of the subject implicate each other:

1. "The signifier is what represents a subject for another "signifier";[12]

2. "The subject is what the signifier represents, and it is not able to represent anything but for another signifier."[13]

Lacan locates this position of the subject in the chain—and, as it were, as the function of its very concatenation, or as the "reason" of this series—specifically in what linguistics designates by the name *shifter*[14] (in French: *embrayeur*).[15] Shifters are, to cite Jakobson, "a special class of grammatical units," whose general meaning "cannot be defined without reference to the message" (namely, in Lacanian terms, to the signifying sequence). The most striking example of a shifter, as Jakobson says, is the personal pronoun: "I" does not achieve its meaning in the code without referring to the message where it can appear as the subject of the statement. But as the subject of the

statement it does not signify the subject of enunciation, it designates it without signifying it.[16] When I say "I," this "I" does not
signify *me*.

Thus the subject staged in Lacan's text—on one level—as
subject of enunciation, must be referred in fact to this other
subject: the one which, caught in the separation between the
subject of the statement and of enunciation, posits or imposes
itself as a pure signifier—or as what a signifier "represents," a
"representation" which is thus not a reference.

We add that, in Lacan, what accomplishes this destruction-
reconstruction of the concept of the subject in the signifier is
the identification of this subject as a subject of game theory,
that is to say—in opposition, in fact, to all subjective identity—as a pure locus, or a pure pivot of a calculus:

> Game theory, better said strategy, is an example of this,
> where one profits from the entirely calculable character
> of a subject which is strictly reduced to the formula of a
> matrix of signifying combinations.[17]

Now, this subject of strategy is none other than the Other
itself (if one may say so): "this Other is simply the pure subject
of the modern game theory"[18] or "the previous site of the pure
subject of the signifier"[19]—that is to say that it "is" the "(-1),"
which we remember is "as such unpronounceable."

The Lacanian subject is instituted, then, in and by the signifier. This is how the pre-inscription of the subject by its "proper" name is repeated and theorized, as evoked in the first page
of the text. The theory of the letter indeed comes full circle [*se
boucle*] in a theory of the subject. The entry into the subject
can then only be an entry into the signifier—while the signified
subject slides outside of itself and its theory comes full circle, in
turn, in that of the letter. Once again, we are led back to the
signifier. The *punctuation* of the subject—consequently, the
punctuation of "*signifiance*" itself—or *signifiance* insofar as it
punctuates—is itself also "mythical" and the Lacanian subject
excludes the substantial subject of meaning [*vouloir-dire*].

At least it excludes it as an existential, psychological, or anthropological subject. For, we must still wonder what, in spite of everything, could possibly be maintained by this maintaining of the *name* "subject," and by the express articulation of a theory of the subject as such.[20]

But in order to move on to this interrogation, one still has to explicate what this theory prescribes with respect to the very functioning of *signifiance*.

We return to our text. The passage through the subject has led us to "the properly signifying function." This function is what the subject articulates, that is, "the representation of a signifier for another," or the paradoxical functioning of signification in the signifier alone. The true function of the subject is one that can be analyzed into the following two elements of connotation: metonymy and metaphor.

(From what has been our point of view until now—and from the point of view of this first part of the text—these two tropes are only going to intervene in order to articulate, with greater precision, a signifying play (a *play* [*jeu*] in place of "I" [*je*]) whose essential rules have all already been stated.

However, from another point of view—that is to say from the point of view of what we will designate as the articulation of the logic of the signifier with Freudian theory—metonymy and metaphor will need to be re-read, insofar as it is in them that the logic of the signifier proves to be a logic of desire, and insofar as this tropology, which seems to close and crown the theory of the letter proper and which draws it entirely into a new order, will take us directly to the articulation in question.)

In Lacan's presentation of these two tropes, we will first take note of what can be designated either as a certain conflation between the taxonomy of classical rhetoric on the one hand, and a Jakobsonian analysis of the two "aspects of language" on the other hand, or as a *figurative* usage in Lacan's discourse of the terms of metonymy and metaphor. Neither, as we will see, is understood within a strict rhetorical sense, nor even an easily discernible one.

Metonymy, first, is introduced by the well-known paradigm of the "thirty sails." These sails are classified by Fontanier as a synecdoche of the part—and thus outside of metonymy. What Lacan has in mind, in fact, with the concept of metonymy, is the series that Jakobson illustates by this trope, the series of the terms of linguistic *combination:* it is discourse as a concatenation of successive entities, as a con-texture of relations *in praesentia,* as a preponderance of conti-guity. Metonymy, thus understood, is the syntagmatic trope, or furthermore, the figure of syntagma.

This figure, in the "same old" (cf. *E.,* 505/156) example of the "thirty sails" may itself be read as a "boat," according to the mischievous play on words in which Lacan encloses the definition.[21] This wily shipwrecking of the classical example serves to emphasize that in the said metonymy, "the thing" is not "to be taken as real"; for a ship ordinarily has more than one sail. The *boat* is thus not the signified of the metonymic twist [*tour*]: it is that twist itself, that is to say the connection of the signifier "ship" to the signifier "sail," namely what Lacan refers to as the *"word to word."*

We will note that this expression can be transcribed into the terms of linguistics which, in fact, it obeys: it is the connec-tion of the signs which produces the figure, not that of the ref-erents. The reality of the rigging of the ship certainly does not form a figure.[22] But by absorbing the signified into this refer-ent, and by discarding both, Lacan wants to eliminate *meaning* along with reality from the figure. The *"word to word"* is the spelling out of the discrete units of the phrase before (or with-out) capturing its meaning, or it is the word-for-word transla-tion which we know does not make sense, or not much, and it is what is more the "word for word," namely the formula of *literality.* This literality which we must paradoxically attribute to the figure is indeed for Lacan the "small amount of mean-ing" [*le "peu de sens"*] described in "The Direction of the Treatment":

> Metonymy is, as I have shown you, that effect made pos-
> sible by the fact that there is no signification that does
> not refer to another signification, and in which their low-
> est common denominator is produced, namely, the small
> amount of meaning.[23]

Metonymy is thus not a figure in the sense of an ornament
or a manner of speaking which would keep meaning *safe*. It is
the syntagma as an axis or twist [*tour*] by which meaning is
impoverished or exhausted in the letter of discourse.

It is thus also the effectuation of this twist, or this blow,
delivered by Lacan, we recall, to Saussurean linearity. The linearity of the syntagma is presumably what is most resistant to
the autonomization of the signifier as conceptualized by
Lacan. This is why metonymy is here, as it were, the twist
which breaks the syntagma and pulverizes it into isolated signifiers, each referring to another signifier, according to a trope
which is nothing other than metaphor in the very broad sense
that Lacan gives it—that is, in the sense of a paradigmatic
trope. (One could also note that Lacan himself, a few years
earlier, namely in "The Function and Field of Speech..." classified metonymy and metaphor as "semantic condensations,"
while "syntactic displacements" were illustrated by another
list of rhetorical terms (*E.,* 268/58). If in *The Agency* the syntactic and the semantic are more conflated than distinguished,
one should presumably understand that it is fundamentally on
the basis of the *trope of the word,* of the figure of *meaning,* or
of figurative *meaning,* that *signifiance* is to be thought as the
exhaustion or exclusion of the signified.)

As for metaphor, the example Lacan borrows from Hugo
via Quillet, "His sheaf was neither miserly nor heinous..." (*E.,*
506/157), seems hardly classifiable as an example of metaphor in
the strict sense: at least two metonymies can be discerned here,
one of the instrumental cause (the sheaf for Booz) and the other
of the effect (the sheaf for the soil or for the savings of Booz).
Above all, what is retained from metaphor is the trait which

establishes the passage from the animate to the inanimate. Quillet and Lacan are therefore faithful to the customary, very broad use of the word metaphor[24]—transport or trope *par excellence,* or production of figurative meaning in general.

"Metaphor" thus applies to Jakobson's other series, namely, the terms which mark language as *selection:* discourse as a concurrence of simultaneous entities, as a substitution against the background of relations *in absentia* or as the preponderance of similarity. Metaphor is therefore the paradigmatic trope, or the figure of alternation by which the message borrows its paradigms from the code.

It is certainly not by chance if, along with the usual meaning of the word "metaphor," Lacan also incorporates the literary genre where we seem to find it most often—namely poetry, and more precisely poetry circumscribed by two references: Hugo and surrealism (*E.,* 506–8/156–58). That is, the poetry that we are able to designate, in its own terms, as that of the Word—of Divine Speech or of speech—and of the "power" or "magic" of words. An entire poetics of this order and an entire poetic practice of this style indeed subtend Lacan's text, here as elsewhere, in its literary references, its peculiar stylistic effects, and finally in its theoretical articulation. The decisive episode of the verse of the *tree* reveals here the recurrence of the specific effects of an intervention of the poetical *into* the theoretical, or *as* theoretical. In this way Lacan's literary references, style or rhetoric are shown to be not merely ornamental, but to belong to the most decisive constitution of his discourse. His discourse—which, while determining the theoretical agency of metaphor, at the same time invites its reader (its auditor) to "produce...a glittering web of metaphors" (*E.,* 507/157)—is a discourse itself woven through and through from a poetics of metaphor.

Metaphor is articulated in the play of substitution of one signifier for another. According to the same logic used for metonymy, Lacan avoids presenting this figure as a procedure which would keep meaning safe. On the contrary, proper meaning—and particularly in the example of Booz, the exemplary sense of the proper name, that is, of the signifier which prescribes a subject—is "abolished." That which is "abolished" never "rises again" (*E.*, 508/158) in person; only a paradoxical return of the abolished through abolition itself can occur, namely in the figure which takes its place. Abolition is thus "nonmeaning" and yet it is that which authorizes meaning: "Metaphor occurs at the precise point where meaning occurs in non-meaning" (*E.*, 508/158).

This nonmeaning, as we see, is to be taken less as *nonsense,*[25] according to the English word for absurd meaning, than as the negative of meaning, a moment of its absence or loss, whose meaning is articulated dialectically. If Booz is exemplary, it is not only as a proper name, but also as the name of a father, namely the one who must be *killed,* in accordance with the "mythical event in terms of which Freud reconstructed the progress in the unconscious of all men, of the paternal mystery," or of "the signification of paternity" (*E.*, 508/158).

The signification of Booz as father in "his sheaf" brings the paternity of all *signification* to light here: it is engendered from nonmeaning, that is to say, outside of the signified, and in the pure signifier. Lacan's formula for metaphor—that is to say for the trope or the play [*tour*] of discourse as a chain of the units of meaning—is the following: "*one word for another*" (*E.*, 508/158).

One word *for* another, this means a word *in place* of another—a substitution of signifiers—but also one word *in view* of another—a sort of internal teleology of the signifying order. This metaphorical teleology is that through which the *subject* insists in the signifier, since it is, we know, "what a signifier represents *for* another signifier"—even if this teleology is bound to perpetuate itself without ever arriving at the *telos* of a substantial subject, a master of meaning.

Metaphor gathers in itself, then, the function of the subject and that of the word; it is the locus where the latter takes possession of the former and "literalizes" it in the form of an odd tropological or signifying literality. The word thus installed in its highest agency is "'the word' *par excellence*": it is Freud's *Witz,* the word that, because it is "none other than the signifier *esprit*" (*E.,* 508/158), is also the letter in its very literality. This *word* is then both the first motif by which Freud intervenes in Lacan's text, and the last element of the theoretical exposition of the letter.

But that letter has yet to pass. What metonymy indicates alongside metaphor is that the "one word for another" must follow the twists and turns of the "word to word" in order to take place. As the "art of writing" in its relation to political persecution, metonymy manifests a "servitude" (*E.,* 508/158) which is inherent in the signifying order, in order for meaning to take place—metonymy itself being the ruse of this servitude.

What is the letter enslaved by? By a *truth,* Lacan tells us. But the enunciation of this truth—on the basis of which the entire tropological play and with it the entire theory of the subject, including the theory of truth to which it relates, organizes itself—draws the entire logic of the letter into a new articulation of discourse, since Lacan names it: The Freudian truth (*E.,* 509/158).

Notes

1. T.N. The word *signifiant,* kept in the French here, is the substantification of the present participle of the verb *signifier* (to signify).

2. T.N. We have rendered the substantified adjective *le propre* as "propriety," which is meant here in the following senses, given by the *OED:* 1. The fact of being one's own, or "ownness." 2. Proper or particular character; own nature, disposition, idiosyncracy, essence, individuality, proper state or condition.

3. *E.,* 840, "Position de l'inconscient."

4. Cf. in particular "The Function and Field of Speech and Language," *E.,* 296/83.

5. T.N. translation modified.

6. T.N. translation modified.

7. T.N. *Grimper à l'arbre* is an idiomatic expression which literally means "to climb the tree," but which has come to mean, "to be fooled," "to have one put over on you." The verb *arborer,* "to raise (e.g., a flag or a banner)," has come to mean "to wear ostentatiously."

8. Cf. Barthes, *Elements of Semiology,* p. 90–91.

9. "The Freudian Thing," *E.,* 409/121.

10. "La science et la vérité," *E.,* 867–68.

11. "Position de l'inconscient," *E.,* 835.

12. For example, "Subversion of the Subject," *E.,* 819/316.

13. "Position de l'inconscient," *E.,* 835.

14. T.N. In English in the original.

15. *E.,* 535/182. Cf. the reference to Jakobson's text that we cite. One should note here that Lacan usually avoids translating the word *shifter,* a solution which is no doubt more appropriate, as much for the "proper" value of this term, as for the usage intended by Lacan. Indeed, it suppresses the "strange automotive metonymy by which Jakobson's French translator makes the shifter (that he translates, we know, by *embrayeur*) slip from a "change in relation" to a "changing of gears" [*embrayage*]. In this way a term that suggests sliding and displacement, is made to connote gripping and anchoring." (Pierre Kuentz "Parole/discours," *Langue française,* no. 15, September 1972, p. 27.)

16. "Subversion of the Subject," *E.,* 800/298.

17. "La science et la vérité," *E.* 860.

18. "Subversion of the Subject," *E.* 806/304.

19. Ibid., 807/305.

20. A certain *maintenance* (conservation and comportment) of the subject will command another turn of reading. Cf. *TL.,* 115.

21. T.N. Lacan's play on the "figurative sense" of *bateau* ("ship" in Sheridan's translation, *E.,* 505/156) has two aspects: *monter un*

bateau à quelqu'un means "to perpetrate a hoax on someone' or 'to pull someone's leg'; and *un sujet bateau* is a hackneyed, tired subject.

22. Even though in Homer's time and often enough in Quintilian's time, a ship ordinarily only had one sail.

23. *E.,* 622/259. T.N. We have modified Sheridan's translation of *"le peu de sens"* ("the little meaning") to emphasize its quantitative connotation.

24. "Metaphor, whose name is perhaps better known than the thing itself, has lost, as Laharpe observes, all its scholastic gravity." Cf. Pierre Fontanier, *Les Figures du Discours* (Paris: Flammarion, 1982), p. 99. To recapture this gravity, consult Gerard Genette, "The Limits of Rhetoric," in *Figures of Literary Discourse,* trans. Alan Sheridan (New York: Columbia University Press, 1982).

25. T.N. Translation modified for reasons which the immediate context will indicate.

26. T.N. In English in the original.

Part II

The Strategy of the Signifier

We have read (or attempted to decipher) the first part of the text, up to the point where, in closing, it refers the *science of the letter* to the "Freudian truth"—which is to say, as one might suspect, to its truth.

We return now to the text:

> But haven't we felt for some time now that, having followed the ways of the letter in search of Freudian truth, we are getting very warm indeed, that it is burning all about us? (*E.,* 509/158)

For the moment we will defer considering the metaphor. This is indeed the moment of an articulation, a strict, classical one—governed, in fact, from the very beginning of the text, by the title itself ("As my title suggests...what the psychoanalytic experience discovers in the unconscious is the whole structure of language" [*E.,* 495/147]). It is an articulation prepared—carefully and progressively brought forth—by a controlled sliding throughout this last page where, in the recapitulation of the general tropism of the letter, Freud's name begins to be heard and, along with it, as a kind of accompaniment to the terminology of linguistics or rhetoric, a few of the concepts of psychoanalysis: *Witz,* censorship, desire.

There is no doubt that this passage develops in an allusive manner—simply a way of indicating here (of coming full circle in order to make the transition) that nothing said about the letter has been foreign to Freud. Nevertheless, a precise logic (tortuous but precise) is at work here, at least up to a certain point, and its movement must be reconstructed, however briefly.

What is at issue is to articulate linguistics and psychoanalysis together. Moreover, it is this articulation itself which founds, properly speaking, what we have called the *science of the letter.* But how can it be accomplished? Or, to be more precise, how can it take place? The text answers: It can take place in a certain relation *between the letter and truth,* insofar as *desire* is implicated therein. This is why there is a shift in emphasis *in fine* toward metonymy (which, as we will see, is the trope of desire). Indeed, metonymy is related to censorship. It is even, for Lacan, the privileged instrument which gives the "power to circumvent the obstacles of social censorship" (*E.,* 508/158). In other words, a forbidden truth is able to be inscribed in the "word to word." Yet this is the heart of the difficulty, in fact, for this simple relation should be inverted. It is not truth which is censored, but rather, on the contrary, it is truth which censors, which founds censorship, or requires it. Moreover, this is why metonymy, like the art of writing, is servile: "Does not this form," Lacan says, "which gives its field to truth in its very oppression, manifest a certain servitude inherent in its presentation?" (*E.,* 509/158). It is no doubt not immaterial that the model of writing reappears here, and that it reappears in the reference to the "conaturality" (*E.,* 509/158) of writing and persecution. Writing loves persecution, as metonymy offers truth the opportunity to exercise an implacable mastery—"an effect" says Lacan brutally, "of truth on desire" (*E.,* 509/158).

For all this to be intelligible one must presuppose, clearly, a truth such that (however hidden, inaccessible, forbidden, and powerful in its very withdrawal) not only does it not give itself, but as it refuses itself, forces the inscription of its very refusal. One should therefore reconstitute an entire theory of truth, and of truth in its relation to desire, by which one might understand that desire, constrained by this inaccessible truth, must necessarily follow a metonymical procession and indefinitely defer itself or indefinitely defer its "end." *Additionally,* one would even have to evaluate the difference between this and the Freudian use of this same "model" of censorship. But this is precisely what is lacking.

Certainly, there will be a return to the motif of the relation between the letter and truth in the next to last paragraph. But it merely takes place through allusion, through the adage in which Lacan recognizes the truth of desire precisely in the letter which "materializes the agency of death."[1] This truth, as we will soon read, is that desire is "a dead desire" (*E.,* 518/167): "certainly the letter kills" writes Lacan, and if, *adage oblige,* this literal death must be opposed to the life of the spirit, it is simply to allow once again the enunciation of the law of *significance* which was developed on the basis of Saussure's work, but this time as that which is proper to the Freudian "discovery."

> The pretensions of the spirit would remain unassailable if the letter had not shown us that it produces all the effects of the truth in man without involving the spirit at all. It is none other than Freud who had this revelation, and he called his discovery the unconscious. (*E.,* 509/158–59)

Thus the articulation is missing.

It is certainly not by chance that, as soon as the word *desire* (to which the articulation must indeed be tied) has been uttered, truth becomes so pressing, the hidden object that had to be looked for so close that "we are getting very warm indeed" as is said in the game called "hot and cold" [*cache-tampon*]. We must now consider this metaphor. For this truth, (whose "revelation" is imminent) is not only what *presses against* [*tamponne*] the letter, but its fire blazes brutally and "engulfs everything." It is well known that the Revelation is inscribed in letters of fire, at least that what is revealed is fire. Here this fire finally burns and devastates nothing other than the articulation itself. In the place where the systematic articulation between Saussure and Freud should occur, it is burning [*ça brûle*], and in such a way that we run the risk of having nothing but the ashes of this constitution of the science of the letter left to decipher.

Whatever the effects of this fire may be, one thing is certain: the textual break which occurs here is so deep and so sharp that henceforth commentary or any simple deciphering is practically forbidden. We must thus rectify the phrase with which we introduced this new development at the start of the chapter. We must not say we have taken the commentary of this first part to the point where the science of the letter is reinscribed in the Freudian truth. Rather we must say that it is impossible to *maintain* a commentary of this text in its entirety, beyond the point where an "articulation" (henceforth in quotation marks) is revealed as it conceals itself, like the truth which founds it. This "articulation," because it proves incapable of fulfilling the function of an "articulation," can no longer be mastered by a commentary, either because it exceeds its resources (thereby producing an economy which is more complex than a discursive one) or because it destroys the whole architectonic edifice in which the commentary is traditionally supposed to take refuge. We have thus taken the commentary dangerously close to the fire that threatens to consume *discourse.* To cross this limit, or even to simply suggest it, would be to burn the commentary. And to say that the commentary is burned can also be understood, in a manner of speaking, as what can be said of informers or intelligence agents.

But can we at least designate the upheaval introduced in the general economy of the text? If the issue of what we have called, for the sake of convenience, "articulation" (or [in] articulation) is to join linguistics and psychoanalysis together, what exactly prevents the articulation from functioning? It seemed, after all, from the beginning, that a simple relation between Freud and Saussure could be established. It seemed sufficient to read linguistics in the light of Freud's discovery. The "articulation" in the end had only to mention something like the *telos* of this enterprise ("I told you it was Freud") in order to produce its possibility *a posteriori.* If nothing of this sort occurs, or at least if something comes to complicate this movement or block this passage, it shows that things are not so simple.

Why? At least for the reason that, throughout this first part, what we have called, following Lacan himself (*E.,* 821/318), a *diversion* of linguistics has never ceased. However, nothing in fact authorizes this diversion, except for a certain use of Freud, a certain way of projecting, more or less explicitly, an entire psychoanalytic conceptual framework into Saussurian linguistics in order to disrupt its operation. And surely, from this point of view, it may be necessary to *re-read* this text so as to locate very precisely the places where psychoanalysis intervenes: a second unavoidable reading of this algorithm entirely constructed upon a resistant bar which can be understood, as we know, as the symbolic bar of repression, a reading which would oblige us to begin again at the beginning, as early as the introduction, under the authority of Saussure.

That second reading is so unavoidable that Lacan himself cannot avoid it, and it is so unavoidable that the second part of the text ("The Letter in the Unconscious") precisely opens with a "linguistic" reading of the Freudian text, which repeats word for word, at least for a time, the Freudian reading of linguistics of which it was nevertheless the condition. This relation is almost indescribable and resists, if not totally refuses, analysis. This is indeed why the articulation does not occur. According to what logic are we in fact to articulate that Freud is to be read according to Saussure, himself read according to Freud? Is this reducible to some dialectic—to dialectic itself? Can we speak in terms of a hermeneutic circularity? And even if we could attempt it, in one way or another, it is precisely what Lacan wants to avoid, or more exactly, what the text does not offer, but rather burns—whatever the origin of this fire may be.

Here, then, we have a twist, apparent in a textual "accident," which modifies the discourse of the letter and which forces its odd repetition: a repetition which, as we will soon see, will have to be repeated *at least* once. For what is lacking in the failure of the "articulation" (or in the lack of articulation), what makes this "articulation" produce, after all, only a pretense of *telos,* is an origin, a foundation, an *arché*. Who *started* it, Saussure or Freud? We will have to examine this lack of origin further, as well as the movement it paradoxically governs. For now, it suffices to note that, if it modifies the course of the text, by the same token it disrupts the commentary.

We will call this duplicitous movement *strategy*. We will begin by explaining ourselves on this point.

Notes

1. Cf. "Seminar on 'The Purloined Letter,'" *E.*, 24/*P.*, 38.

Strategy

Before defining this word we must carefully insist—and all the more so since we will see that many meanings are involved therein—on the duplicity of the movement it designates. In speaking of strategy we in fact have two things in view: on the one hand, Lacan's strategy, and on the other hand, but in a way presumably more complex, something like a certain strategy vis-à-vis the Lacanian text. It is a strategy of *reading,* if you will, since we must abandon our commentary. Not that the issue here is to make war, nor (to use another metaphorical resource which has governed our work from the beginning) to play a bad *trick* [*tour*] on the text. *Strategy* will rather designate the inevitable twisting [*tournure obligée*] of what has been left in the margins of Lacan's text.

This is why, strictly speaking, it will be less a question here of a plurality of meanings than of a certain use, or more exactly, of a multiplicity of possible uses of strategy. And if in fact a plurality of meanings, since it is semantic, always appears as *centered,* then a plurality of uses should be able, with a little luck, to remain relatively dispersed.

But we must begin with "meaning."

At the outset we know that strategy is one of the major elements of Lacanian systematics. Therefore, the word itself is not absent, and if Lacan uses it, he does so (insofar as it is a synonym of game theory) to indicate the possible status of a non-subjective subject—that is to say a plural, combinatory subject, neither present to itself (it is without consciousness) nor in a definite place (since it is reduced to a calculus of odds).

But by appropriating the word in this sense, it is perhaps not impossible to make it designate something else which is relevant: primarily, for example, the mode of composition which could be called the Lacanian "system"—based, it is true, on the sole example of the first part of the text. It is a system made of borrowings or rather, a system of borrowings, which we have seen illustrated in the constitution of a signifying tropism, assembled or fabricated from classical rhetoric, Jakobson's linguistics, post-symbolist or surrealist poetry, etc. Thus, strategy is to be understood here as a technique, or an "art" of systematization—a systematization that does not reveal its own law of composition as an architectural law. Indeed, for there to be an *architectonically* edified system—that is, a *system* in the classical and absolute sense of the term—it must reveal itself as a construction by the positing of concepts. These concepts, if they are not entirely produced in the system, at least display as their laws the rules according to which they have been borrowed from other systems in relation to which they have been reworked. Granted that this architectonic is but a pure ideal of the theoretical, we must at least notice that Lacanian discourse does not define itself in reference to this ideal. As a general rule, his discourse does not posit itself as needing to be defined—rather it seeks to avoid all definitions along with all the difficulties they entail. Moreover, this is what indicates that it comes under another sort of system, more *combined* than constructed. If *strategy,* in sum, is to involve *combination,* it would thus essentially designate two things: on the one hand, a body of procedures of diversion, and on the other hand, the maintaining of the plurality of these procedures as such (and consequently of the domains or areas on the basis of which there is a diversion).

Moreover, it would perhaps be possible to define this *strategy of diversion* in contrast with what contemporary epistemology has designated as the *importation of concepts.* If importation borrows a conceptual unity or feature in order to make it enter into a new systematic game in a regulated manner, diversion, on the contrary, borrows a concept without *working* it—in order to make it serve other ends. By definition, diversion would be *impure*—an impurity such that it could go as far as to mimic or divert importation itself.

Which is to say, in fact—and to use a convenient distinction—that if importation proceeds as a passage from denotation to denotation (and is able to denote the passage itself), diversion is a *connotative sliding.* This will not be without consequences, and this is in any case what allows us to explain that in diversion, the areas of borrowing do not disappear from the horizon of the new system. This is why the latter, instead of presenting itself straightaway as a new theoretical area, sets itself up, if one may say, in an intermediary space, in an intersection of areas or in a permanent circulation between areas. The diverted concepts thus retain the weight of plural reference.

But the idea of strategy always also involves the idea of a finalized or "interested" operation and it is hard to say by what right this should not be taken into account. Indeed, what *interests* Lacan, in the strong sense of the term, is to rescue psychoanalysis from anything that could have, and still could, compromise it, weaken it, deprive it of its "cutting" power or blunt its cutting edge, in the practical and theoretical senses: for instance, perhaps above all, its (political) function of social adaptation, of integration of the ego, etc. (and at least in that respect the political aim is clear)—a danger so pressing and so persistent that it imposes an endless theoretical struggle against all philosophical forms of "subjectivism" at work in classical psychology, anthropology, perhaps even in Husserlian phenomenology and its more or less sentimental derivations.

Hence Lacan's search for what he calls (as early as the preamble, we recall) *formative effects,* a search which commands, on this we must insist, a certain recourse to speech, a certain use of the efficacy proper to speech, and, as it were, of its *persuasive* power. This is in fact what animates and governs the entire Lacanian strategy, and accounts, up to a point, for the scrambling, the turns and disruptions which alter the demonstrative thread of his discourse. A sort of *pedagogical* pre-text keeps working the theoretical text even when it seems absent from it—it keeps *returning,* especially when dealing with Freud, like an emphatic rhythm. The fact that Lacan seeks to rescue psychoanalysis from a certain orthopedics does not prevent, on the contrary, his project as a whole from being orthopedic. It is, if you will, an *anti-orthopedic* orthopedics, or a counter-pedagogy, which is not unrelated, in its critical intention as well, to perhaps the most fundamental aim of philosophy as a whole, at least since Socrates. Lacan's *formation* would thus be nothing else, presumably, than παιδεία itself, or its revival in the *Bildung* of the Enlightenment (with which Lacan explicitly affiliates himself)[1] and of German Idealism. One would even have to include that second theoretical "accompaniment" of philosophy associated, most of the time, with the pedagogical project itself, that is the *medical* accompaniment. For formation is formation for psychoanalysis, formation of the psychoanalyst, even if it is not reserved exclusively for practitioners alone, that is to say for *medical doctors* alone. This explains why psychoanalysis could appear, here, as a sort of *generalized* medicine, the *paideia* of all *paideiai,* the paideiac procession, if one may say, which would be henceforth unavoidable. Thus the psychoanalyst would have three functions, as Lacan says, that of the "scientist," the "mage," and the "quack," [*mège*] (*E.,* 521/169).[2] Lacan's address, delivered at the University and within academic discourse, was authorized by this three-fold function.

What matters here, no doubt, is that this motif of formation (but it is more than just a motif[3]) allows the Lacanian strategy to be presented according to a *specular* model (where theory aims at the formation of the psychoanalyst who, as he practices psychoanalysis, in turn, renders theory possible), or even according to the just as rigorously and profoundly philosophical model of the *mise en abyme*—a *mise en abyme* where Lacan's *style* is necessarily implicated. The path of the "return to Freud," as is said at the end of "La psychanalyse et son enseignement," is "the only formation that we could claim to transmit to our followers. It is called a style" (*E.,* 458). And why a style if not by virtue of a "circuit" whose course we could drily reconstitute by invoking the notion that if theory engenders the concept of a subject which regulates the subject of psychoanalysis, the latter consequently is able to institute itself as the subject of discourse, in other words, to take the place of Lacan himself, or if you will, of the one who trains the subject of psychoanalysis. When Lacan speaks it would thus be the Other who speaks and speaks about him.

Evidently, this is only one of the possible courses. What we are proposing here regarding strategy remains schematic and hasty, and no doubt one should read, for instance, a text like "The Direction of the Treatment," very closely, at least in its first two divisions. But we did not want to break the rule that we have tried to follow up to now, and which obliges us to limit, as far as possible, incursions beyond the text we have chosen to read.

However, we have said enough to suggest that it is neither desirable nor even possible to extricate ourselves from such a strategy, and that, consequently, one must necessarily *read* the text according to the demands or requisites of strategy itself. This is why it is out of the question to *criticize* Lacan, which is to say, to exercise the systematic jurisdiction of *discourse* itself on his discourse. We will see that this excludes, in particular, reproaching him for any unfaithfulness to epistemological rigor or holding the liberties he takes with scientific linguistics against him.[4] On the contrary, our reading should follow the diversions and displacements with which Lacanian discourse is woven, following or accompanying them, adhering to their complex design as closely as possible. This is not to say that we should purely and simply repeat them (devoutly), but rather that we should interrogate the logic of his discourse, that is, its

strategic intention, in order to measure its "displacing" efficacy
and the excess which emerges there in relation to science and
philosophy.

Obviously, the promise of such an excess makes Lacan's
discourse lend itself to a strategy which is carried out on its
own strategy, granted that one can ultimately maintain the
form of this reduplication. But strategy itself is discursive; it
necessarily belongs, and has always belonged, as such, to the
philosophical order of discourse. War is *philosophical* and
whatever its destructive power, it always maintains itself within the limits of the philosophical, and it even maintains those
very limits. We should thus have recourse to something which
is neither a strategy of a strategy nor, clearly, a counter-strate-
gy. Therefore, for obvious reasons, we shall speak of deconstruction, if deconstruction, which is indeed discursive and
strategic, nevertheless always gravitates as it were in excess of
itself and does not cease to undo the discursive and the
strategic within itself. We will thus also oppose the text,[5] as we
indicated, to discourse, even if it proves necessary, now and
then, to complicate this distinction, or more exactly, to adjust
it to the form it takes in Lacan's work. Indeed, it may well be
(as mentioned previously) that as Lacan conceives it, the text
is nothing but discourse itself, impeccable and circular, that is,
the signifying order as such *and* as it is itself inscribed in
Freud's work (or even in Lacan's insofar as he admits, as well,
to having the "text" in view), in brief, nothing other than truth
in its *logos*. It may well be that speech, on the other hand, is
itself for Lacan the (incomplete) text, the perpetually suspended "discourse" of initiation, incitement, and exhortation,
which is suited to stimulate, put into play, or puzzle, can never
achieve a *knowledge* of truth. The difference between strategy
and what we have in mind here would perhaps depend on the
difference between two forms of *excess:* Lacanian excess,
which alters discourse or to which discourse submits, to the
point of inarticulation (as it would submit to the unbearable
surge of a truth too powerful and too eager to *express* itself

[*de vouloir se dire*] to *be able* to do so [*pour pouvoir se dire*]—the "fire" mentioned earlier would be an example of this) must be distinguished from a reading which meticulously overflows the banks of the text (or of the discourse...) that it undertakes to read,[6] and which would privilege these moments of overflowing which come to agitate and steer, now and then, the course of the text.

In this sense, we are henceforth bound to strategy, that is to say, to deconstruction. The overflowing of the text requires it. It will be a question, precisely, of *re-reading*. If the overflowing which appears in the (in)articulation disturbs the text, if it produces a certain tremor in the discursive edifice, if it displaces, however minimally, its pieces or its parts, we must now follow the fault lines and persist not in sketching the map, the founding and structural architecture, but rather in tracing the guiding thread that alters it.

Now as we saw, the principle of this second reading commands, for its own reasons, the very economy of the text. If, in sum, the lack of articulation is a sign, it is because it paradoxically exhibits the odd circularity between Freud and Saussure, and compels the repetition of a reading of Freud which is itself a Freudian reading of Saussure. We thus have to follow this second navigation in its turn. This is why our strategic reading will begin with the motif of *repetition*.

In one sense, nothing distinguishes the work we are now beginning, at least in its first "moment," from the deciphering we attempted with respect to the first part of Lacan's text. Quite simply we will attempt to decipher repetition (or comment on it, which amounts to the same thing). An identical task, then, though not as slow, since after all, the essential results have already been well established; or nearly so.

But in fact things are not that simple—and besides, we know quite well that repetition is not the reduplication of the identical. Lacan's text cannot help but submit to that very law. This is why repetition here is not actually *simple*. Indeed, as soon as its necessity has been inscribed in the text (and we know now that this occurs as early as the beginning, or even *before* the beginning of the text—if that is conceivable—as its most rigorous prescription), the disequilibrium introduced there causes repetition to flare up, repeat itself anew, and to never cease repeating itself. This is an infinite process, that only a *coup de force* could possibly interrupt—and only provisionally. It will take the form not only of an explicitly linguistico-Freudian repetition of Freud (if one can put it that way), but also of an openly philosophical repetition of this very repetition, insofar as a whole philosophical design, explicit at times, was indeed already working the Freudian diversion of linguistics and was attempting, perhaps, to present itself as the principle, the solution (the sublation?) of the infinite exchange which relates Freud and Saussure.

Thus it is not surprising that the whole second part of the text ("The Letter in the Unconscious") is first preoccupied with the spectre of this relation. The peremptory tone should not mislead us. Neither the introductory declaration ("In the complete works of Freud, one out of every three pages is devoted to philological references, one out of every two pages to logical inferences, everywhere a dialectical apprehension of experience, the proportion of analysis of language increasing as the unconscious is more directly concerned" [*E.,* 509/159]), nor such and such a proposition on the "lead" of the Freudian formalization over the formalizations of linguistics, would in fact allow the question to be avoided (*E.,* 512–13/161–62). And we know quite well that it still awaits an answer.[7]

Consequently there is no "solution," but, on the contrary, a repetition of the very gesture with which the reading of Saussure was initiated, and with which the reading of the *Traumdeutung* (not accidentally translated as the *signifiance du rêve,* as we already noted) will begin. It is necessary indeed to take the "letter to the letter," and because in the *Traumdeutung,* "every page deals with what I call the letter of the discourse" (*E.,* 509/159), it is necessary to take the letter of Freud to the letter, to read Freud to the letter—which amounts precisely to (re)reading the letter in Freud. The title, "The Letter in the Unconscious," speaks for itself.

The principle of this (re)reading is twofold: on the one hand, since the point is to discern "the agency in the dream of the same literalizing (or phonematic) structure in which the signifier is articulated and analyzed in discourse" (*E.,* 510/159), one must recognize the essential features of a pure play of the signifier, distinct from any analogical symbolism, in the models used by Freud (the rebus, hieroglyphic writing); on the other hand, and more precisely, the point is to identify the elements or functions of the letter itself, in all the elements of the *dream work.* Consequently, both principles imply that one substitutes deciphering for decoding and that instead of a simple pantomime or symbolic imagery, one recognizes a genuine "system of writing" (*E.,* 511/161) in the dream, understanding that it is indeed the phonetic model, that is the ideal, in sum, of alphabetical writing, which regulates this concept of writing.[8]

Hence the *literal* transcription of the major elements of Freud's conceptual apparatus. To recall the essentials:

1. *Enstellung* (that is, depending on the translations, "transposition" or "distortion") should be interpreted by what has been "designated earlier with Saussure" as the sliding of the signified under the signifier.

2. *Verdichtung* (condensation) refers to metaphor;[9] *Verschiebung* (displacement) refers to metonomy.

3. *Rücksicht auf Darstellbarkeit,* "the taking account of figurability" (what Lacan translates by "consideration for the means of representation [*mise en scène*] and what, according to Freud, (*The Interpretation of Dreams* chap. 6, 4) is a process accompanying the work of condensation and displacement that makes the figuration of the dream contents possible) is irreducible to the order of the image and instead should be understood as dependent on a "system of writing."

4. Finally, secondary revision is either insignificant insofar as it belongs to the conscious process, or else it provides ele-

ments that come to be integrated in the signifying play of unconscious thought (that is, strictly speaking, of the dream-thoughts, *Traumgedanke*) (*E.,* 511–12/161).

Consequently, once the translation of the Freudian lexicon has been assured, or if one prefers, once it has been confirmed that Freud indeed speaks the language of the science of the letter, then not only does it become impossible to read, in the text of the *Traumdeutung,* the experimental novel of a psychical unconscious (that is to say the psychological novel of the unconscious); but one can only (re)discover a pure functioning at work there which can be formalized according to the rules of linguistic formalization itself. "It is a matter, therefore, of defining the topography of this unconscious. I say that it is the very topography defined by the algorithm" (*E.,* 515/163). This is a formula which, once developed according to the principle of "the effects of the signifier on the signified," is able to engender the formulas of metaphor and metonomy. Namely, those three successive formulas which in fact cannot be read as genuine logical formulas (they neither suppose nor authorize any calculus here), which Lacan transposes as follows.

1. The general formula:

$$f(S) \frac{I}{s}$$

which can be read as, the function of the signifier is to posit a term on a bar resisting signification.

2. The formula of metonymy:

$$f(S \ldots S') \cong S(\text{---})s$$

which can be read as, the signifying function of the inter-connection of signifiers is equivalent to the maintaining of the bar which holds the signified out of the signifier's grasp. The "elided" signified is then able to designate the object of desire as "*lack* of being," a lack by which desire is doomed to function as the deferral, along the chain, of the metonymy of this lack.

3. Finally, the formula for metaphor:

$$f\left(\frac{S'}{S}\right) S \cong S\,(+)\,s$$

which can be read as, "the signifying function of the substitution of a signifier for another signifier is equivalent to the crossing of the bar (hence the sign $+$)[10] in the creation of signification." The signification thus produced is a poetic effect of signification. In other words, it belongs to the order of connotation, where it is immediately subjected to the permanent sliding of the signified. It is this passage which previously had permitted the designation of the place of the subject.

Now it is precisely here that another rupture takes place. A rupture itself produced by the repetitive constraint which henceforth necessarily governs the text. It is not by chance, therefore, that Lacan underscores it in the following way:

> This crossing expresses the condition of passage of the signifier into the signified that I pointed out above, although *provisionally* (our emphasis) confusing it with the place of the subject.
>
> It is the function of the subject, thus introduced, that we must now turn to, since it lies at the crucial point of our problem. (*E.*, 516/164.)

What was therefore working the whole first part of the text, to the point of defering the crossing of the bar practically to the end, now undermines the repetition of Freud itself, since the question of what the first part had succeeded (provisionally, says Lacan) in considering as the "passage in the subject," of the *presence* of the signifier in the subject, remains to be settled (cf. *E.*, 504/155). Now Freud's text itself (or more exactly, by itself) is not sufficient for a return to the question of the subject. Thus it is necessary to go through another text which is distinct from both the Freudian and the linguistic texts—the philosophical text. This repetition of the repetition begins with Descartes.

We must indeed begin again with the *cogito*. It is *also* therefore the *cogito* that we must subvert (referring to the title of another of Lacan's texts, "Subversion of the Subject and Dialectic of Desire," which guides, at least in part, the philosophical itinerary that we are now going to cover), since the same logic is here again at work. To subvert the *cogito* means essentially to reduce it and exhaust it, to the point of retaining nothing but the pure position of the subject as such. Therefore it also means to "desubstantialize" it, according to a quite classical gesture (but which is here accentuated), since Lacan not only takes issue with the psychological depth that a certain tradition thought possible to retain (after having imported it into the Cartesian *cogito* from elsewhere), but also with the pure self-transparency of transcendental subjectivity, insofar as it maintains the subject within the horizon of presence-to-self in general. This is why, on the one hand, it is necessary to establish a link between the *cogito* and the subject of strategy (or of game theory, or else of a combinatory order alluded to above in the diverted logical formulas), and on the other hand, to "excenter" the subject in relation to the classical subject.

It is obviously Freud who permits us to acknowledge this excentricity of the *cogito*. But it is still necessary to understand that not only is the Cartesian foundation indispensable to measure the gap introduced by psychoanalysis, but that the excentricity which Freud sought to exhibit in the relation of the subject to itself, is in fact only formulable in linguistic terms—namely, in terms of the difference between the subject of enunciation and the subject of the statement. Hence the twofold formulation of the Freudian "*cogito*" (and the duplicity is necessary here), "I am not wherever I am the plaything of my thoughts; I think of what I am where I do not think to think" (*E.,* 517/166), which derives in fact from the retranscription of the Cartesian formula: "*cogito ergo sum*" *ubi cogito, ibi sum* (*E.,* 516/165). This retranscription reveals the difference between statement and enunciation. It is this difference which can be understood as the introduction—at the heart of the subject it splits or crosses out [*barre*]—of the desire which emerged empirically in psychoanalytic "experience," a desire defined by nothing other than its locking onto a refusal of the signifier (hence the necessity of metaphorical substitution) or onto a lack of being (hence the necessity of metonymical displacement, to which the incompletion of desire is bound).

The system of repetition can now be considered to be in place. This is precisely why the mechanism of repetition will accelerate. The comings and goings between the three texts (linguistics, psychoanalysis, and philosophy) will accelerate as if by the effect of a rapid oscillation between the two edges of a gap. In a way, nothing new will occur. But this "nothing new" actually contains the possibility of a proliferation of philosophical references. For if the relation between Freud and Saussure remains blocked, the only possibility of introducing a disequilibrium capable of making one of these two "terms" move is to emphasize the insistence, whether explicit or not, of the philosophical. It is this new turn taken by the text which will lead us now from Descartes to Heidegger.

Schematically, this process can be analyzed in three moments:

1. The Freudian "machine" definitively takes the place of the subject. Metaphor and metonymy (which linguistics had posited in the place where the subject was to be produced), once transposed into Freudian conceptuality, form "mechanisms" therein which submit the subject to the machinery of the "other scene." Indeed, in metaphor "the symptom is determined" as the substitution of a corporeal signifier for another repressed signifier, a substitution which renders "signification inaccessible to the conscious subject" (*E.,* 518/166). As for metonymy, it carries desire as a perpetual "desire for something else," thus dooming desire to be given as always already dead, caught in a purely mechanical memory. This memory then allows us to understand Freudian repetition insofar as it solves

the *aporia* of philosophical reminiscence. For, if this reminiscence runs into the insurmountable difficulty of having to invert the meaning of a process of generation,[11] Freudian repetition, being "mechanical," takes the form of a displacement of desire onto an "other scene" which is not originary. The subject is thus the tool of this machination, or the tool with which "being poses its question" (*E.*, 520/168). This being is nothing other than the being that desire lacks, and which for that reason "only appears in a lightning moment in the void of the verb to be" (520/168). It is a pure effect of the signifier, therefore, and hence capable, through the "resistances proper to the signifying pathway of truth," which is to say according to the *rhetoric* of the unconscious,[12] of producing the signification of the subject as a narcissistic resistance of the ego.

2. This entire functioning can thus be understood as "the radical excentricity of the self to itself with which man is confronted" (*E.*, 524/172). This excentricity calls for a "mediation," which is that of the Other. As we already know, the Other is what institutes the contract of speech, and it is at this point in the text that Rousseau's name is inscribed between the lines[13]—as is Hegel's, if the Other indeed "indicates the beyond in which the recognition of desire is bound up with the desire for recognition" (*E.*, 524/172): that is to say if the Other appears as the mediator of a dialectic, which would be properly Hegelian if Lacan did not brutally reduce it to a contractual relation.

3. It remains then to grasp what is proper to the Freudian "revolution." Its formula is quite simple—whatever the subtlety of the detour of the example of Erasmus which allows its production:[14] it consists in removing the unconscious from the domination of consciousness and in tearing madness away from the hold of *logos*.

> Madness, you are no longer the object of the ambiguous praise with which the sage decorated the impregnable burrow of his fear; and if after all he finds him-

self tolerably at home there, it is only because the supreme agent forever at work digging its tunnels is none other than reason, the very Logos that he serves. (*E.,* 526/174)

In its simplicity, or even in its obviousness, this formula could close the text. It "points" indeed to the situation of "reason since Freud," namely, to the "agency of the letter" itself, and it consequently names "an immense truth in which Freud has traced for us a clear path" (*E.,* 527/174).

Yet this is not at all what occurs. Far from ending, the text continues a bit longer. One more page, in fact, where everything is put back into play. For the truth of the Freudian discovery is referred there to another truth, which in principle one did not expect: the Heideggerian truth, which is, as everyone knows, *aletheia.* But, as we suspect, the relation of one to the other is not simple: it is indeed so complex that it might involve a logic which is irreducible to the logic of repetition that we have followed up to now, thus risking overflowing it—and constraining us, consequently, to defer its analysis, at least temporarily.

This is why we will limit ourselves, for the moment, to emphasizing two things:

1. The sudden appearance of Heidegger's name, at least because of the surprise it provokes, indeed seems to belong to the series of disruptions and accidents which have constantly derailed the simple logic of Lacan's itinerary. More profoundly, to the extent that Heidegger here indicates "a re-examination of the situation of man in the midst of beings such as has been assumed up to the present by all our postulates of knowledge" (*E.,* 527-8/175, slightly modified), his intervention seems to threaten all the philosophical resources which have been used in this itinerary.

2. On the other hand Heideggerean truth seems to *accomplish* the logic of this text. Indeed, the letter is from the start

related to *being,* which must be understood as that of the Heideggerian "question" of "being." Finally, it is to this "question" that metaphor is "bound"—or better, it is in the formulas of the science of the letter, where the vocabulary of linguistics and psychoanalysis are combined, that the Heideggerian signifier of *being* comes to stamp the seal of its truth.

> For the symptom *is* a metaphor, whether one likes it or not, as desire *is* a metonomy, however funny people may find the idea. (*E.,* 528/175)

Therefore we must include this truth—*aletheia*—within the logic of Lacanian strategy before being able to say what such an operation produces in the calculus of the whole. To that end, we must first examine the functioning of this whole as such.

Notes

1. Cf., for example, the introductory note of the *Ecrits.*

2. The quack is nothing other—must we say it?—than the one who cares for: in old French, *mégier,* "to care for," derives from the Latin *medicare.* T.N. Translation slightly modified.

3. If only because it probably involves, in the final analysis, the question that one could designate under the very general rubrics of 'psychoanalysis in the political' and 'the political in psychoanalysis.' Obviously such a question cannot be elaborated here. We can only indicate that the Lacanian strategy might perhaps allow access to its problematic complexity. In any case, the question cannot be reduced to some simple 'politics of psychoanalysis,' any more than to a no-less-simple 'psychoanalysis of politics,' whatever their respective references or preferences.

4. As well as with Freud's "text."

5. We refer here, generally, to Derrida's work as a whole and more specifically to the clarifications in "Positions," *Promesse,* no. 30/31, Fall/Winter 1971, reprinted in *Positions,* trans. Alan Bass (Chicago: University of Chicago Press, 1981).

6. The constraints of a twofold metaphor are at play in this dis-

tinction. It is impossible not to notice it here. On the one hand, fire, the solar overflowing of light, on the other hand (rather) water, flooding—and first, no doubt, *infiltration*. But one will understand that we do not say more on this here, since it would be necessary, in all rigor, to trace fire back to the father (to man), and water, perhaps (but only perhaps), to the mother (to woman). It would then remain—but this exceeds our intentions—to weave all this into the motif which seems to govern, at its end, a text like the "Signification of the Phallus" "Correlatively, one can glimpse the reason for a characteristic that had never before been elucidated, and which shows once again the depth of Freud's intuition: namely, why he advances the view that there is only one *libido,* his text showing that he conceives it as masculine in nature. The function of the phallic signifier touches here on its most profound relations: that in which the Ancients embodied the Νοῦς and the Λογός " *E.,* 695/291.

7. We here allude, for example, to "Radiophonie," p. 55, where the answer appears in a no-less-problematical form in the formula: "The unconscious is the condition of linguistics," p. 58.

8. Hence the insistence with which Lacan notes Freud's use of the presence of the *determinative* in hieroglyphic writing [Freud, *The Interpretation of Dreams* (1900), *S.E.,* IV, 329], in order to emphasize that "the value of the image as signifier has nothing whatever to do with its signification..." and "to show that even in this writing the so-called 'ideogram' is a letter," *E.,* 510/159–160.

9. That *Verdichtung* refers to metaphor, and thus, through it, to "poetry," is also indicated in the "condensation" produced from *Dichtung.* This is a homonymic call which could not be justified in any way, says J. F. Lyotard in "The Dream-Work Does Not Think," trans., Mary Lydon, *Oxford Literary Review,* v. 6, no. 1, 1983, since the *Dichtung* of *Verdichtung*—"condensation" or "thickening"—has no etymological link with the "speaking" [*disante*] *Dichtung* of fiction or poetry. This remark is a *critical* motif in relation to which one can mark the singularity of the reading we are attempting here, especially when dealing with Lacan's interpretation of Freud, which we do not have to pass judgement at this point, for reasons which by now should be obvious.

10. The "ideographic" discrepancy of this mark in relation to the usual symbol of addition—a discrepancy which has every appearance of a *Witz* on logico-mathematical notation—shows the extent of the diversion produced here at the expense of logic.

11. As is still the case in the Hölderlinian law of the return; but not in Kierkegaardian *repetition.* "Starting from the Hölderlinian νόστος Freud arrives less than twenty years later at Kierkegaard's repetition," *E.,* 519/167. This allusion at least permits us to understand that in this journey, a certain submission to the simple law of a unique *logos* ("the sovereign principle of the Logos" according to Hölderlin's terms retrieved here) gradually gives way to an irreducible dualism ("the Empedoclean antinomies of death," with which Freud, as we know, explicitly affiliated himself).

12. "Periphrasis, hyperbaton, ellipsis, suspension, anticipation, retraction, negation, digression, irony: these are the figures of style (Quintilian's *figurae sententiarium*); as catechresis, litotes, autonomasia, hypotyposis, are the tropes, whose terms suggest themselves as the most proper for the labelling of these mechanisms," *E.,* 521/169. Cf. Benveniste, *Problems in General Linguistics,* p. 65.

13. Cf. *TL.,* 31.

14. "So how do you imagine that a scholar with so little talent for the 'commitments' that solicited him in his age (as they do in all ages), that a scholar such as Erasmus held such an eminent place in the revolution of a Reformation in which man has as much of a stake in each man as in all men?

The answer is that the slightest alteration in the relation between man and the signifier, in this case in the procedures of exegesis, changes the whole course of history by modifying the moorings that anchor his being," *E.,* 526–27/174.

Erasmus is thus the ambiguous panegyrist of madness that we cite next. Yet his obedient submission to the Logos could not prevent him (on the contrary, if in fact reason freely enters into the disorder of madness), in altering the signifier of the Book (of the Letter), from subverting occidental reason and wisdom.

2.

System and Combination

Strategy is thus what orders and governs this complex of inter-woven repetitions. We must now exhibit this strategy for itself, or manifest its specific effects. That is, we must reread Lacan's text or repeat its reading, as we will see, several times.

Strategy here is to be understood as a *comprehensive strategy* that Lacan's entire text obeys, both in its economy and structure—or more precisely—to which his text owes its economy and structure, in the literal sense of these terms, that is, in their "restricted" sense. According to this comprehensive strategy, the text simultaneously espouses a twofold motif—a duality or duplicity which is, as we know, the very element of strategy, and the reason for the repetition of reading.

Indeed, on the one hand, this text performs a sort of *combination* of borrowings, perversions, subversions or repetitions by which it institutes itself. In this respect its movement corresponds, on the whole, to what we called a procedure of *diversion*.

But this diversion, the nature of which remains to be grasped, itself makes use of yet another movement—a *turning movement*, if you will—by which, in the very course of Lacanian discourse, in its ruptures and suspensions, something installs, accomplishes, and encloses itself with all the characteristics of *systematicity*.

We must attempt to discern this twofold movement and decipher its law. This means, of course, that we will have to come to the following question: Is this strategic duplication maintained to the end, is it the twofold "locus" of Lacan's text?

Or does one of the sides in fact turn into the other? That is, does diversion go as far as *diverting the system* [*détourner le système*] which seems to be (re)constituted in Lacanian discourse? Or, on the contrary, does such a (re)constitution *turn* the diversion itself *into a system* [*retourner en système*]? Unless, of course, this alternative itself proves undecidable.

We are able to begin reading the strategic effects of this discourse with these questions, starting with *systematicity* [*effet de système*].

The construction produced in the first part of *The Agency,* and the repetition of this construction through a whole series of theoretical motifs and agencies has already revealed that it is a systematic text (that is, a "discourse" in the strong sense). We must now dwell on this systematicity, that is, on the *discourse* held by Lacan's text, insofar as, conforming to the fundamental and foundational requirement of scientific and/or philosophical discourse, it accomplishes itself by itself in a self-enclosed order. This order includes nothing that is not organically "articulated" within it, and excludes nothing from its circumference without ordering it according to that very circumference. Any system is then the system (that is, in Greek, the *combinatory position*[1]) of a certain self-identity of the "articulation" of discourse: it is the "*archê*" and the "*telos*" of a *logic.*

We will permit ourselves, having "spelled it out" in our reading, to bring this systematicity into *view* in the schema proposed here.[2]

But we will not comment on this schema without first prefacing it—as if to duplicate it—with two texts. First, since—as we just recalled—systematicity is Greek, and proceeds from an imperious demand of discourse, this passage from Plato's *Epinomis,*[3] whose elements and entire logic circle continuously at the perimeter [*pourtour*] of our schema:

> This is the turn (τρόπος)—for it is necessary to state at
> least this: all things described and figured (διάγραμμα),
> all systems of numbers (ἀριθμός), all combinations

(σύστασις) of harmony and the homology of the revolution of planets, all this must fully exhibit its unity for
those who learn according to the turn.

Consequently, another text will circle here as well, which
could be (which is indeed, although it is not its explicit aim) the
commentary of the preceding one. With respect to a certain
point on the perimeter of our graph, it is not unimportant that
this one is by Heidegger.

> The system is not at all simply nor first an ordering of
> the available matter of knowledge—and of what is
> worth knowing for the purpose of the accurate commu-
> nication of this knowledge—rather the system is indeed
> the internal articulation [*Fügung*] of the knowable
> itself, the unfolding and the formation [*Gestaltung*]
> which found it, and more properly still: the system is
> the articulation conforming to the knowledge of the
> conjunction [*Gefüge*] and the junction [*Fuge*] of being
> itself.[4]

Whatever these introductory inscriptions may lead us to
think (or invite us to believe), for the time being such a schema
clearly cannot have any other claims than those of any graphic
representation in which the graphic itself is not the place or the
object of a scientific process or of a calculus. Thus there is
nothing geometrical or topological here, only the quite empirical appearances of convenience and recourse to sensible intuition. In this regard it cannot exempt itself from its commentary. Our use of such a figure is, then, for us, only a game. (This
disclaimer is necessary since such schemas are taken so seriously in a culture still haunted by the *mos geometricum*.) It simply
happens that this game, like many others, is instructive.

The use of a schema is undoubtedly not unjustified in our
reading, nor irrelevant to the text to be read. To bring the systematic unity of this discourse into *view* is perhaps first only a
manner of *repeating* the unity that was meant to be *understood*

[*entendre*] in the event of its enunciation. The schema would then be the repetition—just as "literal" as "metaphorical"—of the resource that Lacan's speech (as implied in the preamble) draws from the occasion of a "discourse" in the oratory sense, that is, from a single grasp, a direct (if not simple), immediate, and for that reason sensible apprehension offered to a university audience before being offered in the *Ecrits,* which is, one should not forget, "a title more ironic than one might think."[5]

This schema can then sustain itself through a conformity to the procedure—no less "playful"—of graphic representation used by Lacan in other texts,[6] without these "graphs" having the slightest congruence with mathematical graph theory. The Lacanian "graph" also belongs to the strategy of diversion.

We will thus attempt a spatial representation of this strategy (mimicking its procedures somewhat) in order to examine the form it permits—or demands. It so happens that this form is that of the *circle* and, up to a certain *point* at least, that of the *flawless* or *remainderless* circle. This is the form of the *ring* Lacan speaks about when, using yet another game, he evokes the "elusive ambiguity" according to which "the ring of meaning flees from our grasp along the verbal thread" (*E.,* 517/166)[7]—which means that if the ring of meaning flees, it still does so along another ring, that of the circle of players.

This circle—if we first consider the smallest circumference of the schema—can be made to turn from any one of its points. For instance the *letter* itself is what, as it institutes itself as the materiality of a place, pre-inscribes the subject "in its place," which is that of a signifier. But the letter is also that which is instituted only through the Other, whose contract inscribes the letter in speech, that is, in the capacity for truth (characterized, as we saw, by adequation—*adaequatio* or *homoiosis*—to which we will return).

But the same letter is inscribed—and withdraws—in an *aletheia,* an ultimate truth, which the text obliges us to take account of as the "Freudian truth," that is, as that truth which oppresses desire. This is a truth that the subject cannot *know* and that amounts to the signifying gap of (in) speech, or better, that is identified by enunciating itself as such a gap or *hole.* In this gesture *being* comes to be lacking three times on the circle: from speech (*metonymy*), through speech (*metaphor*), and in speech (the verb *to be*). As lacking, being occupies another place of the Other—an *Other scene,* which is thus the same and, for this reason, on the circle's rim. From that place, being governs—through the letter and its circuit—the *subject* which closes the literal circle with its absence.

As for the circumference itself, it will suffice to have thus set it in motion. Anyone can then see it close itself on any of its points, each punctuating, as it were, the "same" absence, the "same" alteration, or altering its identity in an identical way.

The interior of the circle repeats the closure of its outline. This interior is indeed divided by the very division of speech, that is to say by the *hole* that the letter hollows out with its circle. Therefore speech only "crosses" the bar, which is resistant to signification, by substituting for the first signifier (the one under the bar) the metaphorical signifier (the one above the bar, which is always-already there and which, since it takes the place of another, is rendered as S$^{\prime 9}$). The latter is itself immediately swept into the metonymical chain. Consequently, speech allows for the indefinitely open, twofold series of the slidings of the signified (in the order of metaphor, governed by the *machine* which, from the other scene, deprives the subject of both its place and propriety) as well as the connections of the signifier where the "small amount of meaning" of a *desire* oppressed by truth insists (that is, in the order of metonymy, governed by this localization of the letter which assigns to the subject the "place" where it is deprived of itself).

But this irreducible duality is also what fills in and closes off the circle, through the symmetry which henceforth can be located on both sides of the bar. Being, whose lack is metonymized by the chain, is that which slides in a "lightning flash" outside of its own verb. The name of the subject is that which, as signified,

"System" of "The Agency of the Letter," or:
De revolutionibus orbium litteralium[8]

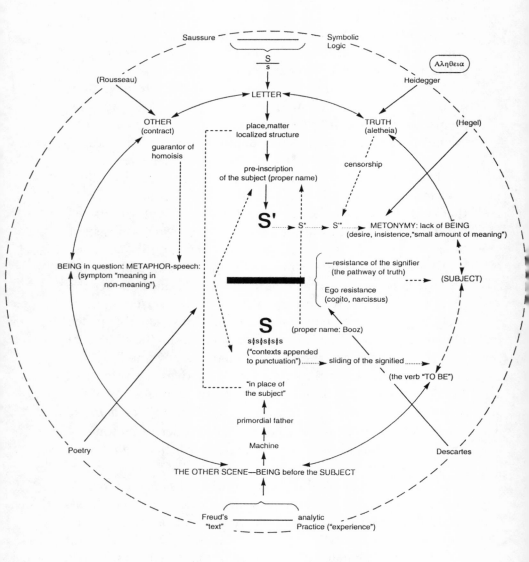

is abolished. The place of this paradoxically pre-inscribed (pre-proscribed) subject is held by the operation of the machine. And the machination of the murder of the father is none other than that of the substitution of the signifier. Hence, the place of the machine, Freud's "other scene" in which "the machine directs the director" (*E.,* 519/167), is the scene of the Other, that is to say, once again, the circle of the letter—the circular scene where the letter puts its agency into play.

The process of speech in its twofold series has, additionally, a "direction" [*sens*]: it goes towards nomination and the signification of the subject (the genitive, here, being both subjective and objective). But the subject which is produced in the crossing of the bar—that is, through a double play of resistances, that of the signifier oppressed by truth and that of the imaginary signified—can only be a subject *which does not come into being,* and which in turn is nothing but a point on the circumference, where it lacks being and where the letter divides it (this is why the arc which supports it is traced in a broken line, yet does not detract from the closure of the circle).

The circularity of the circle is thus:

- the symmetry of the operations of speech,
- the symmetry of the "literal" and "unconscious" organization,
- the identity of all the cardinal terms on the circumference which govern all these symmetries.

To which we must still add:

- the identity of the circumference itself and of the operations it includes.

The terms of the circumference indeed behave toward each other as *metaphors* in Lacan's sense of the term: the letter, truth, the Other, being, and the subject form a system here to the extent that the function of each consists in coming to its "place" *for an other*; and the circular chain of these functions,

ruled by the position of the non-coming into being of the subject (or of being...), is indeed a *metonymical* chain.

But the circulation of such an "identity" requires, for its
circle, a *center*. It is in this necessity of the center that we can
see the figure of the schema exercise the most decisive constraint on what it figures. Indeed, to the extent that such a
graphic offers a convenient yet accurate account of Lacan's discourse, that discourse proves, by the same token, to be
circular—that is to say systematic. But it also proves to be *centered,* even though the graphic could not inscribe (and should
not have inscribed) this center as such.

Indeed, the bar crosses the center. By making the central
point "burst," the bar should also shatter the identity of the circle and disrupt its functioning to the point of precluding any
meaning of the term *system*. However, this meaning does take
place. *At least* as a system, Lacan's discourse, as we hope to
have just shown, reduces the gaps that it hollows out and
comes to a halt on its own sliding (or stops its sliding by giving
it the form of the circle). In this stopping, it centers itself—and
this center is the bar itself, whose thickness serves thus to con-
ceal a point. This is the very point of the system, its punctuation: that is, the *concept* from which it is possible to order the
elements and the relations of *a logic of the signifier* which is,
thus, without diversion, a *logic* pure and simple.

One must recognize in this punctual (and punctuating)
value of the bar what Lacan's discourse has posited as a principle: the bar is *foundational* or *originary*. It is the *archê* of a system which, while systematizing the division, the lack, or the
hole in the places of origin, has nevertheless maintained its
own "*archaic*" value of systematicity—that is, of origin and
center—without questioning it further. Clearly Lacan's
thought, despite its effects of dispersion or dislocation, does
not exclude a discursive exposition, nor consequently a unitary
and monological arrangement. It even commands such an
arrangement, unless it happens to be commanded by it.
Despite everything that, by virtue of the signifier, opposes it,

there is a systematic force at work in the "logic of the signifier" that does not cease to reconstruct or recenter what Lacan's critique of "monocentrism"[10] aims at destroying or exceeding.

In this sense, the bar which functions as a center is able to engender another circle: namely, the circle circumscribed by the circle of the system, which serves as its origin. The bar is what traces or constructs the algorithm by treating Saussure and symbolic logic in terms of one another; it is what repeats Rousseau in a contract of speech, draws its resources from a poetics of metaphor, assigns Descartes to the place of the impossible subject, and Hegel to the law of desire. The bar, finally (or first) is what brings Freud and Heidegger into the same circle, the former to give an empirical and scientific basis to the bar before its time, and the latter to indicate the mode of truth of such a theory.

All these (proper) names circulate, in turn, according to the law of the first circle: they are metaphors of one another, in a kind of synchronic projection and indefinite repetition of the history of Western thought (we should not forget, moreover, all those names from Plato to Hölderlin that the text has mentioned); they thus constitute the circle of *reason* "since Freud" and their chain metonymizes the theory or the system of the letter. Yet the *telos* of this metonymy *is* in fact achieved, since it is this system itself or at least its possibility which is inscribed as the law of the discourse held here. This is also why this system, just as it has a center, also has a proper name: that of Lacan.[11]

In all these respects—that is, in *only one* respect, that of the center, or that of the function of a center fulfilled here in spite of everything—Lacan composes a system in the most classical sense of the term. The Lacanian revolution, which borrows the image of the "Copernican revolution"[12] from Kant via Freud, perhaps *also* proceeds contrary to that revolution. Instead of distending the circle into a bifocal ellipse—one of whose foci, moreover, would be empty—it leads back to a circular revolution. This is why the schema could be entitled with a parody of

Copernicus's title, which must be understood in the following sense: the letter of Lacan's text (we will carefully retain the equivocity of this expression) produces its effects according to the concentric turns of a literally systematic discourse.

If Lacan was able to say that his "statements have nothing in common with a theoretical exposé justified by a closure,"[13] we see at this stage of our reading that this declaration ought rather to be understood in terms of the difference between an effect that is produced and the will to destroy or subvert this very effect. This is why, moreover—as we mentioned earlier—it is not certain that this system simply functions as such, as system. Indeed, to the extent that its systematicity is produced in a combination of multiple diversions, what is important is to determine the extent to which the function of diversion diverts or disrupts systematicity. At least it is not unimportant, in this respect, that a system bar its center, even if this bar is *also* nothing but a point.

A twofold reading of this "system" is thus necessary; we must turn the page of the schema, not, however, without taking note of what is retained in reserve there and which we will treat of later: the inscription of *aletheia* that had to be doubled—once Latinized on the rim of the circle, another time in Greek outside of it. In order to read this double inscription, we must reconsider Lacan's entire strategy and discern whether the inscription is duplicated by it or outside of it, because of it or in spite of it.

Another approach to the system, this time considered as a combination of displacements, will allow us first to discover a new duplication: combination radicalizes the aim of the system and at the same time attempts to exceed it. We will proceed progressively.

Strategy was thus initiated by a certain treatment of linguistics. That treatment is a diversion, as we have seen, in the sense that it uses Saussure while radically criticizing him, and attributes an algorithm to him which he knew nothing about. Additionally, metaphor and metonymy, borrowed from Jakobson, have lost their characteristics as complementary "aspects" of language (whose respective preponderance may vary, according to literary genre, for example) and have become two autonomous entities whose association constitutes the law of language as the law of desire.

The aim of that entire treatment, we know, was to relate the linguistic function to Freud—but to a Freud himself deciphered in linguistic terms. This is an obscure circle where we saw the "articulation" or the (in)articulation of Lacan's text take place. We will return to this "articulation," but only though the long detour that we begin here.

Indeed, for the moment we can simply make the following observation: properly speaking, there is no basis on which we can reproach Lacan for lacking linguistic rigor. He cannot be criticized by linguistics any more than he formulates his "critiques" of Saussure as a linguist (they are rather gaps, or slidings, indifferent to their possible critical scope). He transcribes linguistics entirely in Freudian terms: this transcription is, at least up to a certain point, removed from linguistic authority. (This confirms our suggestion that strategy, as such, evades *critical* jurisdiction and offers itself to another movement, a movement which both confirms and disassembles strategic operations).

It evades criticism, but on the other hand, a question arises: why are the concepts and lexicon of linguistics, although transcribed, maintained at least in part?[14]

The answer is that, in the diversion and in the relative blurring of concepts resulting from it, something must indeed be maintained which belongs less to the content of the linguistic discipline than to what founds and delimits it, both in its Saussurean stage and in the later stages which fundamentally derive from it. This "something" could presumably be outlined in many different ways by recourse to diverse moments of Lacan's text. But we can at least designate the element which, on two occasions, his theory endows with an essential determination: namely, the *subject.*

Indeed, the entire linguistic apparatus is diverted above all in order to (re)produce the gap between the statement and the enunciation. In this gap, the linguistic *shifter* comes to accommodate "the matrix of signifying combinations" to which the "subject" is reduced—that is, it accomodates as well the entire process of this subject: "the entire dialectic of desire and the network of the marks that it shapes are hollowed in the interval between statement and enunciation," as is said in a text that is not by Lacan himself, but which is present in a volume signed, "properly speaking," only by the name of Lacan.[15]

The *shifter,* a singularly remarkable property in linguistics, is thus diverted into an irremediable gap between statement (the order of marks and inscriptions) and enunciation, which is the impossible identification of the speaking subject: on the one hand, marks, letters, and literature as well, on the other hand, the unlocatable author or speaker. But this gap, as we know, is also caused by the *letter* which divides speech as soon as it opens it, and thus splits its subject—or, as it splits the subject, divides its speech.

In one way or another this gap [*écart*] clearly takes its value in relation to what one parts from [*s'écarte*], or to what is torn apart [*écartelé*] at the heart of a present subject. This impossible subject and that unassignable locus are the negative reference of the literal gap, but they are also its constituting moment, or for that matter, its substrate. They are *impossible,* but the signifying order is not *possible* without their "presence" in the gap which hollows it out (and which it hollows).

Thus one sees what has been retained from linguistics, even in its diversion: that from which it proceeds and which governs it, namely, the model of the subject of a consciousness transparent to itself in its significations, and whose linguistic underpinnings, long recognized and interrogated (or reduced) by philosophy, are belatedly explored, scientifically, by linguistics. This model constitutes Saussurean linguistics, among others, as a linguistics *of speech* (and therefore of communication).

The philosophical motif of linguistics is thus transposed

into the logic of the signifier. Here the subject falls into a hole, yet this hole is nevertheless delineated by speech, which remains intact, as it were.

This is how we might characterize the first moment of the strategic combination. We note, in passing, what constitutes the formal rule of the following operations: the rule of a *twofold* gesture with respect to the diverted element, destroyed each time in the same move.

Linguistics is the object of yet another displacement. It is combined with a general system of scientificity whose status has never been recognized by any epistemology modeled on the exact sciences. Yet it is through logical formalization and Bachelardian epistemology that, for Lacan, Saussure becomes the founder of a "science in the modern sense" (*E.,* 497/149). Here the situation is complex. On the one hand, Saussure, who produced no algorithm, remains a stranger to any formalization in the logical sense. On the other hand, epistemology is far from relying exclusively "on the constitutive moment of an algorithm" for all science. Strictly speaking, such is only the case for logic. But the epistemology of logic has the peculiarity of merging with logic itself, particularly in the modern epoch when the latter becomes "algorithmic" or "symbolic."

Thus it would seem that Lacan, thanks to these interwoven displacements, installs his science of the letter in place of a circularity where logic only pertains to itself. This is indeed what occurs, in a way, according to the "logic" of this scientific foundation.[16]

In fact, it is not a question of using logic as an instrument—this would condemn the science of the letter, given its radicality, to repeating all the problems that logic stirs up when, in order to establish itself in truth, it must refer outside of itself, thus opening the question of the "meaning of meaning" as the diverse empiricisms or logical positivisms have been able to formulate it, and as Lacan, specifically, refutes it (cf. *E.,* 498/150).

Rather, the issue is to conform to logic in its self-normativity at the point where, in order to make itself decidable, it is instituted as a *science of logic,* according to Hegel's title, or is produced as that *characteristic* sought by Leibniz, which was meant as a universal writing of "figures which are significant by themselves."[17] In any case, the fundamental project is the same and aims at reducing the sign in its duality and opacity. The ideal of a pure language, paradoxically foreign to the play of signification, is one with that of a divine calculus which is the measure of a φωνή σεμαντική, creator of the world and of the sign itself.

Certainly, Lacan will consider this logic in light of the failure of its closure or of its decidability, in the "failure of the effort to suture (the subject of science)" which is demonstated by "Gödel's last theorem."[18] But we know that this theorem can be considered—or interpreted—precisely as the fault whereby logic, "lacking" a "mark" of its completeness, must convert that lack into a metaphysical resource (or distress). As long as it remains dependent on such an interpretation, it remains metaphysical logic in the modern sense.[19] Clearly, we do not have to take part in this debate. It suffices that this interpretation—the most "classical one" and, moreover, that of Gödel himself—is also Lacan's, that is to say that the logic he invokes is, in a negative sense, the "science of logic" itself, or the "science" of the abyss of logic, or even the divine calculus of an absent God.

However, this logic is not simply taken into account by Lacan. Calculus is precisely for him the object of the most avowed diversion. Indeed, it is with respect to calculus that Lacan introduces the term *diversion:*

> ...at the risk of incurring a certain amount of opprobrium, I have indicated to what point I have pushed the diversion of the mathematical algorithm for my own ends: the symbol $\sqrt{-1}$,[20] which is still written as *i* in the theory of complex numbers, is obviously justified

simply because it makes no claim to an automatism in its later use.[21]

Clearly then, since he admits it, Lacan's logic is not serious:

> What is called logic or law is never more than a body of rules that were laboriously drawn up at a moment of history.... I shall expect nothing therefore of those rules except the good faith of the Other, and, as a last resort, will make use of them, if I see fit or if I am forced to, only to amuse bad faith.[22]

And this is indeed why the formulas of "congruence" which *The Agency* gives for metaphor and metonymy, as well as the entire algorithmic process and all the calculations it may engender, are to be taken between the game and the feint, Lacan himself forbidding that one be taken in by them.[23]

But this determination of a sort of logical parody is neither unique nor univocal. First, Lacan's formulas vary, and, as we have been able to see, the entire algorithmic of *The Agency* is apparently presented in the name of the most "serious" science. Next, even though the parody might be concealed here for circumstantial reasons, one should still wonder: isn't it precisely a negative "science" "of logic" that authorizes and calls for its parody? A negative science but still a science *of logic*?

We will not respond immediately to this question. Rather, we will note as a third strategic moment that the motif of science is at least taken "seriously" in the sense that "reflection on the conditions of science" once more produces, at its "historical highpoint," the "function of the subject" which is "at the crucial point of our problem" (*E.,* 516/164). We must now dwell on the philosophical foundation of science—in the twofold value of the genitive—that is to say, on Descartes's *cogito*.

We have seen that this *cogito* exemplified, as a "philosophical pretension" (*E.,* 516/165), "the mirage that renders modern man so sure of being himself" (E.517/165). It is the resistant Narcissus uprooted by the Freudian subversion in view of an essentially ambiguous end: "This end is one of reintegration and harmony, I could even say of reconciliation" (*E.*, 524/171). This is how Lacan interprets Freud's "*Wo es war, soll Ich werden.*" But this reconciliation must take place within the "radical excentricity of the self to itself with which man is confronted" (*E.*, 524/171). This twofold status of reconciliation governs the twofold treatment of Descartes.

Indeed, the "philosophical pretensions" should not serve "to elude" the *cogito*. Far from being taken out of the game, the subject rather rules the game:

> For the notion of subject is indispensable even to the operation of a science such as strategy (in the modern sense) whose calculations exclude all "subjectivism." (*E.*, 516/165)

If the substantiality of the *cogito* is challenged, Descartes, on the other hand, is maintained in two respects: a punctuality of the subject, and a decisive—even deciding—relation to science as calculus. Lacan refers to Descartes' *Discourse,* but we know one need only read *The Regulae*[24] to discover, at the foundation of the *cogito* itself, a subject who is articulated in and by mathematics. It is thus Descartes himself, as it were, or the essential articulation of his discourse, who is *both* excluded *and* repeated.

More curiously still—or more strategically—he is repeated twice: a first time in the notion of the resistant *ego,* which "Freud introduced into his doctrine" (*E.*, 520/168), and another time in the statements which compose, finally, what Lacan names "the two-sided mystery" (*E.*, 518/166) of the subject, which we already mentioned: "I am not wherever I am the plaything of my thought; I think of what I am where I do not think to think" (*E.*, 517–18/166).

One sees that these formulas are indeed statements that displace or dislodge the subject, but which nevertheless are enunciations of an *I,* through which this *I* conserves the mastery of a certainty which, in spite of its contents, yields nothing to that of the "I think." Even the gap of the *shifter* operates almost as a sort of confirmation of the subject adhering to its own certainty through the certainty of its noncoincidence to itself.

The "radical excentricity" of this subject must itself be understood according to this twofold relation to Descartes. The subject is certainly 'excentered' from the circle, or from the sphere of subjectivity—but it is also an *excentric,* that is to say, a "mechanism conceived in such a way that the axis of *rotation* of a driving part does not occupy its center" (Robert). This subject nonetheless remains the *driving force of a rotation.*

The subject is excentered by its desire—or its desire can only be an excentric process. When it is a question of desire, it is Hegel who intervenes in the text, albeit anonymously.

We will not go so far as interpreting this anonymity as a murderous metaphoricity on the part of the father of this text. We shall nevertheless wonder whether it is not because of its excessive proximity that his name must be silenced, insofar as it is in relation to him that the twofold strategic gesture is most prevalent. He would then share this status with Rousseau, another "name" that *insists* in the text, and to which we will return.

Be that as it may, and to the extent that it is possible and necessary to clarify what is implicit in *The Agency* with regard to Hegel by referring to some of Lacan's other texts (and they are numerous, but we will only cite a few of them[25]), we can bring at least the following to light:

The excentricity of the Lacanian subject is always posited in reference to Hegel. In other words, it is in reference to "Hegel's insistence on the fundamental identity of the particular to the universal," an insistence that reveals the measure of his genius, that "psychoanalysis...offers its paradigm by revealing the structure in which that identity is realized as disjunctive of the subject..."[26] This formula indeed indicates the twofold relation to Hegel that is at stake here. It is constructed in order to exhibit the exemplary accomplishment of the Hegelian dialectic of consciousness in the psychoanalytic "subject." At the same time, what it ultimately asserts—the disjunction of the subject—serves to break that dialectic, or rather to suspend its course before its completion.

Indeed, what Lacan refuses in Hegel is the totalization of this "logicizing *Aufhebung*"[27] according to which "truth is in a state of constant reabsorption in its own disturbing element,"[28] and where, consequently, the "unhappiness of conscious-ness...is still no more than the suspension of a corpus of knowl-edge"[29] —of absolute knowledge, to which, moreover, the sub-ject of the signifier cannot have access.

Nevertheless, as the first citation indicates, one must begin with the Hegelian dialectic. It is what engenders, in *The Agen-cy,* the binding of the "recognition of desire" with "the desire for recognition" (*E.,* 524/172), which was expressly attributed by Lacan to its author.[30] And we must come to that dialectic, or rather remain in it, if "the dialectic that underlies our experi-ence...requires us to understand the ego from one end to the other in the movement of progressive alienation where self-consciousness is constituted in Hegel's phenomenology."[31] The law of the process of the subject will always be formulated "lit-erally" in Hegelian terms. Hence the text entitled "The Sub-version of the Subject and the Dialectic of Desire" will con-clude with a phrase that makes explicit the subjection of desire to the truth which arose in the (in)articulation of our text: "Castration means that *jouissance*[32] must be refused, so that it can be reached on the inverted ladder of the Law of desire" (*E.,* 827/324).

As we can see, to say that Freud suspends dialectic or to say that Hegel can be read as a dialectic without completion amounts to the same thing. Or, more precisely, it is the same process of alienation or negativity which can no longer "sim-ply" be understood in reference to the Absolute, but rather to the Other.

It is in this respect that dialectic permeates *The Agency of the Letter.* It qualifies, there, the Freudian "apprehension" of "experience" by touching the "analytic of language" with its meaning (*E.,* 509/159), it gives the formations of the unconscious "their most secret attraction" (*E.,* 513/162), and finally, it is the "dialectic of the return" from which "Freud derives all access to the object" (*E.,* 519/167). Whether or not these occurrences are strictly Hegelian (and how could this be determined if Lacan refuses or avoids the exposition of the concept?) one sees that the Hegelian signifier circulates in the text and even though it slides, its signified finishes by being punctuated in the *mediation* which is repeated three times on page 524/172. Indeed, that mediation is rigorously Hegelian, since this "psychoanalytic mediation" is due to the Other, which is "in the position of mediating between me and the double of myself."[33]

No doubt, this anchoring point undoes itself, at least in the other signifier that accompanies it—the *"heteronomy"* discussed on pages 524/172 and 525/173. This term would, in turn, refer and be quite close to Bataille's "heterology"—by virtue of which a well-known subversive repetition of Hegel would obliquely insert itself in Lacan's text.[34] Here, as at all those points where an *impossible* intervenes in Lacan's work, Bataille's strategy would not be foreign to that of the "letter." But in spite of everything Lacan's maintenance—his presupposition—of a mediation which is simply posited and assumed allows us to extract a name from the text which is even more hidden than Hegel's.

The fact that the dialectical mediation is retained—or that we are faced in this text with a certain dialectical *maintaining*—requires us to ask this question: is the "beyond" (*E.,* 524/172) of the Other fundamentally other than the *other* of Hegelian desire? When, in Hegel, consciousness discovers that the suppression it desires for its satisfaction implies that the "other also ought to be," it realizes the following: "It is in fact an other than self-consciousness which is the essence of desire."[35] And this alterity (which we must, obviously, not interpret in an anthropological sense) commands the structure, if you will, of *jouissance:* "...*jouissance* fulfilled has indeed the positive significance that self-consciousness has become objective to *itself*; but equally, it has the negative one of having sublated *itself*."[36]

We should add however, since we have to follow all the detours, that Lacan would object to the absolute knowledge ultimately supposed to bring this process to its end. But, if "Freud, by his discovery, brought within the circle of science the boundary between the object and being that seemed to mark its outer limit" (E.527/175), hasn't Lacan in fact concluded the science of the letter with a Hegelian formulation which is not unrelated to absolute knowledge?

We shall let the passage speak for itself. Lacan's diversion of Hegel first consists in turning the dialectic of desire (and thus of knowledge) into a negative discourse. Lacanian dialectic thus governs a constant disappropriation of the subject against the background of absence and division by the Other, whereas Hegelian dialectic governs its process of appropriation against the background of presence and the reduction of alterity. As we saw, the *end* of this dialectic nevertheless remains, in Lacan's work, an end "of reintegration and agreement" (*E.,* 524/172). And the principle of its movement is in fact Hegelian: mediation and, thus, *Aufhebung.* Finally and perhaps above all, if in Lacan this principle remains affected by a negativity which seems to resist the positive conversion driving the progress of the stages of consciousness in Hegel (or if, in other words, it is a question here of an *un*-conscious), such a determination will not prevent the constant possibility and necessity of wondering whether that negative discourse is not already *prescribed* by Hegel and *comprehended* by his discourse. This is a discourse that no simple negativity can escape from, as it is precisely within it that the discursive status of negativity is decided.[37]

Nevertheless, Hegel's discourse is in turn taken beyond its limits. The mediation of the Other slides towards the contract of speech (*E.,* 524/172), which leads us to Rousseau.

With respect to Rousseau, we have seen that the difficulty

relative to the anteriority of language was settled by Lacan. By the same token, the contract is assigned the position of principle or *origin,* in contrast to the constant oscillation which maintains *The Social Contract* between political project and foundational ideality. (We know that Rousseau admits, at the beginning of the *Contract,* to being incapable of describing a history, that is, for him, an origin).

If the motif of contract is one way of putting the simplicity of origin into question—-or at least in suspense—one must then say that Lacan himself oscillates between a Rousseau re-read in this way (though not explicitly) and a Rousseauism as a metaphysical contractualism.

Now, this contract is a "signifying convention" (*E.,* 525/ 173)—which means that the treatment of Rousseau is repeated within the theory of the sign. "The origin of language," if you will, refers for Lacan to the "kernel of our being," an expression borrowed from Freud, and to which the rhetoric of the unconscious "attests" (*E.,* 526/173). This rhetoric is primary because there is a *propriety* which (behind it, instituting or founding it as *rhetoric* or *tropism*), remains inaccessible: "that which...creates my being" is not "that which can be an object of knowledge" (*E.,* 526/173).

This is how Lacan's strategy comes to culminate in an operation carried out on the metaphysical theory of the sign. His epigraph, we recall, metaphorized repressed language as a language of children and affects. Let us cite Rousseau: "One would be led to believe that needs dictated the first gestures and that passions brought forth the first voices."[38] What Lacan's epigraph metaphorizes could *just as well* be Rousseau's text, with the difference, certainly, that the sign destroyed by Lacan has lost its referent, its propriety [*son propre*]: or rather, that its property [*propriété*] has been reduced to referring (itself) to a hole. But is the property of reference itself, or of its principle, consequently dislocated? Nothing is less certain. On the contrary, we see that something like an inverted "Rousseauism" can still be deciphered in the diversion of contractualism, and, in place of an "Essay on the Origin of Languages," a "Treatise on the Other('s) Original Language."[39]

With this last operation,we can gather together the results of this entire itinerary, along which, through borrowings and slidings from one scientific or philosophic agency to another, Lacan produces the combination of his letter. The ambiguous relation of reference to the hole gives it its structure:

A subject in the hole, calculated by a vanished God, turns according to an excentric rotation that delineates the circle of its science, that is, a negative dialectic of its desire, sealed by the contract of speech that refers to the hole—such "is" combination.

Such is the apparatus that reveals the "measure" of "the ontological dignity" (*E.,* 513/162) that Freud (according to Lacan) and then Lacan himself grant "this object": *The Agency of the Letter in the Unconscious.*

And this is indeed an ontology, as one might expect after having seen strategy borrow so many elements for its combination from the major history of metaphysical ontology: all the essential features of the latter are present here to the point that the extended formula of combination should be that of an onto-theo-semio-logy.

Clearly, this is a *negative* ontology, since its center is designated and its circumference delineated by a hole—that hole in front of which one must "have one's eyes" (*E.,* 500/152). But the contour of the hole is nevertheless the path of an ontology, an ontology where the *letter,* which lacks "being," "delineates" "the edge of the hole in knowledge," as Lacan himself says when refering specifically to *The Agency.*[40]

It is an ontology that opens onto—and is founded (that is, closed) on—a gaping hole whose bottom is hidden but whose outline can be discerned. Such a motif is not without precedent in the metaphysical tradition, notably as "negative theology." The ultimate effect of Lacanian strategy, at least in that it is a

strategy of system and combination, thus turns out to be a surprising but rigorous repetition of negative theology—that is to
say of what Hegel (him again) had already repeated and displaced.[41] And with Hegel we happen to come even closer to
Bataille. Unless, precisely, we note that a Lacanian atheology,
in accordance with the process of its production, would retain
the epithet "metaphysical" in its strategic ambiguity, and thus
would be a "negative atheology."

Taking account of this doubled negative, then, leads us
back to Hegel. However if it is a question of *reading,* we must
then decipher what distinguishes a negative theology from an
"atheology" in Bataille's sense. But let us remain in the *discursive* writing of Lacan's text just a while longer.

Thus we return here to the twofold aim which opened our
itinerary. One sees that Lacan's strategy radicalizes the system.
The latter is not only what a schema might attempt to render as
a closed field bordered by reference; it is also a combination
which institutes a more secret and a more fundamental closure
(and on which the first depends), the repetition of the most
determinative philosophical demand (or philosophical will or
desire) with respect to discourse: the aspiration to a system or
the constraint exercised by systematicity insofar as they represent a *logos* entirely founded and articulated by itself, or insofar as they express the will of the Self (albeit an "ego" whose
identity is constantly abolished in the imaginary and in the sliding of the signified) to appropriate itself as discourse.

In a way, the duality that organizes this entire strategy is
itself organized in the duplication of discourse (which is also a
reduplication of the discourse of metaphysics) by which philosophy has always sought to be its own concept in a language
proper to it.

This concept, here, is that of "being." But this language is
instituted by the letter—a language with holes in it which
divides being, a language which, when it seeks to combine the
major terms of its discourse, can only be uttered in an *(in)artic-*

ulation. (In)articulation is thus also the singular order of this unique ontology that we thought we could (re)articulate. In this way, Lacan's metaphysical discourse immediately throws itself outside of itself, outside of the ontological closure within which it is nevertheless rigourously inscribed. We can now begin to take account of what manifests such a desire.

For the letter belongs to Freud—to a "subversive" (*E.,* 517/165) power that threatens the whole of philosophy; and being belongs to Heidegger—to the enterprise of the destruction (*Destruktion* or rather, according to the meaning of the term in German, *deconstruction)* of ontology.

It then remains for us to exceed or to swerve toward the twofold exterior of ontology. Unless the issue is to complete the re-reading of our schema in a circular fashion by closing it with the names of Freud and Heidegger, left in suspense until now.

Duplicity repeats itself. Strategy is not yet accomplished. Perhaps it is just now beginning. After all, we have still said nothing about its *truth....*

Notes

1. This translation indicates the fine and fragile difference between *system* and diverting *combination.* The stakes of the text— its double turn—are to dwell in this difference, and perhaps to displace it.

2. Cf. *TL.,* 110.

3. Plato, *Epinomis* 991e. The well-known debate as to whether or not this text should be attributed to Plato "himself" is irrelevant here. T.N. We have followed Lacoue-Labarthe and Nancy's translation.

4. Martin Heidegger, *Shelling's Treatise on the Essence of Human Freedom,* trans., Joan Stambaugh (London: Ohio University Press, 1985), p. 28.

5. "Lituraterre," in *Littérature,* no. 3, p. 4.

6. Cf. *E.,* 48, 50, 53, 56–57, 548/192, 571/212, 673, 674, 680, 774, 778, 805/303, 808/306, 815/313, 817/315. We also find it in various places in unpublished seminars. The necessary precautions relative to the nature of these "graphs" have been taken by J.-A. Miller, *Cahiers pour l'analyse,* no. 1/2, 1966, p. 171.

7. This elusiveness persists in Lacan's work: cf. *E.,* 259/50.

8. Cf. *E.,* 401/114, 506/156, and "Radiophonie," p. 82.

9. Cf. the formulas of *E.,* 515/163–64, already cited.

10. Cf. the "necessity of humbling the arrogance of all monocentrism," that we cited earlier on p. 8 of this work.

11. As is marked, now and then, in this text or in others, by the inscription of his name in his discourse, or by the frequent use of the first person, a *shifter* which, *in spite of everything,* anchors the statement in the enunciation, and reciprocally.

12. See the references of the schema, and *The Agency,* p. 516/165.

13. Cf. *TL.,* 8.

14. Or, if you prefer, what is the status in Lacan's work of such a *maintaining,* in itself no doubt unavoidable? Diverting *and* maintaining: what relation does this play [*tour*] have with "suppressing and conserving" in the Hegelian *Aufhebung?* This is another form of the question of the system.

15. "Pour une logique du fantasme," *Scilicet* no. 2/3, p. 238.

16. Here we neglect the other model, that of the foundation of an experimental science about which Lacan drops a few hints when he speaks of psychoanalytic "experience." These hints connoted rather than denoted, refer to a diversion of the scientific concept of experience—but they remain too vague and too often suggest an appeal to an *empirical* authority of "experience" for them to deserve any more attention.

17. Gottfried Wilhelm Leibniz, *New Essays on Human Understanding,* trans., Peter Remnant and J. Bennett (Cambridge: Cambridge University Press, 1981), IV. 6.2. Should we recall that the first (and last) model of the characteristic is an *Ars combinatoria?*

18. "La science et la vérité," *E.*, 861.

19. This is one of the results of A. Badiou's analysis devoted to Gödel's theorem in Lacan's work, in "Marque et Manque: à propos du zéro," *Cahiers pour l'analyse*, no. 10. Our work only intersects with Badiou's on this point—perhaps then, accentuating its relevance. Let us note moreover that Badiou's article can be read as an analysis of Lacan's discourse which is inverse to yet symmetrical with ours, the fold of this symmetry falling between a question addressed to logic (or to science) and a question addressed to the text.

20. This symbol has just designated the signified in its relation with the (-1), which we have already cited, and with the signifier of a lack in the other (a metaphorical "root"...).

21. "Subversion of the Subject," *E,* 821/318–19. T.N. Translation slightly modified.

22. "The Freudian Thing," *E.,* 431/140.

23. Cf. "Subversion of the Subject," *E.,* 819/317, 821/318, and "Radiophonie," p. 68.

24. As well as the general commentary on the *cogito,* whether Gueroult's or Heidegger's.

25. One would have to examine the history of the relation between Lacan and Hegel—certainly a decisive one for a philosophical deciphering of the discourse of *Ecrits*—including Lacan's vehement rejection of Jean Wahl who had labeled him a Hegelian ("Subversion of the Subject" *E.,* 804/302): this text would deserve a careful reading. T.N. With respect to Lacan's relation to Hegel see Mikkel Borch-Jacobsen's *Lacan: The Absolute Master,* trans., Douglas Brick (Stanford: Stanford University Press, 1991).

Although this is not the place for it, on the other hand it is perhaps the place to at least emphasize the following. It has been written that "Lacan...only rewrites Hegel and Freud, which does not deserve so much fuss [*bruit*]," P. Trotignon in *l'Arc* no. 30, p. 30). That it does not deserve *fuss* is certain. But that nothing happens in a "rewriting," or that what happens is only simple, is far from obvious. Lacan would not be worth reading if nothing were at stake in this rewriting, that is, if there were not *also* a question of knowing the stakes of Hegel's and Freud's texts, among others (how or whereby they pass, how they move, are diverted or circumvented, are led back to the same or are reinscribed elsewhere, and also to what extent, through which channels, these texts have or have not governed the various readings made of them today, etc.)

26. "Function and Field," *E.,* 292/80.

27. "Subversion of the Subject," *E.,* 795/294.

28. Ibid., *E.,* 797/296.

29. Ibid., *E.,* 799/297.

30. Cf. "Propos sur la causalité psychique," *E.,* 181.

31. "Introduction au commentaire de Jean Hyppolite," *E.,* 374.

32. T.N. Here we follow Sheridan in leaving *jouissance* untranslated.

33. It is on this basis that one must presumably understand the "immediacy" of the unconscious, referred to on page 518/166–67. We refer the reader to Hegel's "sense certainty."

34. But it is not by chance that Bataille did not choose *heteronomy,* as he dismissed *heterodoxy* due to its appeal to *orthodoxy,* (Cf. Georges Bataille, *Oeuvres Complètes* [Complete Works] (Paris: Gallimard, 1970–1988), p. 424, no. 12) This is a simple sign of what would separate Lacan from Bataille.

35. G. W. F. Hegel, *Phenomenology of Spirit,* trans., A. V. Miller (Oxford: Oxford University Press, 1977), p. 109. Translation slightly modified.

36. Ibid., p. 218–19, translation modified. In this experience, Hegel continues, "the attained reality of self-consciousness sees itself destroyed."

37. One could, moreover, wonder why Lacan did not have recourse to Marx's reading of Hegel (in the 1844 Manuscripts) as a "process without a subject," a reading currently reactivated from diverse perspectives. Does Lacan see too well that this *process* is already, by itself, *the subject*? Or is he on the contrary so fascinated by the *subject* that he does not see what he retains of it when he tries to distance himself from Hegel?

38. Rousseau, "Essay on the Origin of Language" in *On the Origin of Language,* trans., John H. Moran and Alexander Gode (Chicago: University of Chicago Press, 1966), p. 11. T.N. Translation slightly modified.

39. This would be more clearly brought to light if we could here consider the Lacanian theory of the *real,* that impossible real, but a *real* nonetheless, which is ultimately what is at issue for the subject, for its desire and for *signifiance.* But this would entail commenting on other texts: for example the "Réponse au commentaire de Jean Hyppolite." *E.,* 369–299.

40. "Lituraterre," in *Littérature,* no. 3, p. 5.

41. That is to say, perhaps, of what Lacan has called a *Dio-logy,* a discipline distinct from *theoria* (which is theological, whether "Christian" or "atheist"). A *Dio-logy* precisely designates negative theology or mysticism: "It seems to us that it is still Freud who best indicates the place of *Dio-logy...* whose fathers range from Moses to Joyce to Meister Eckhart." We find it, in Lacan's work, in "a theory which includes a lack to be retrieved at all levels," ("La méprise du sujet supposé savoir," *Scilicet* no. 1, pp. 39–40.) One would thus have to read this entire text, which assigns among others "the place of God-the-Father" to the question of the "Name-of-the-Father" (p. 39), namely to the question whose exposition Lacan, since his expulsion from Sainte-Anne, has wanted to defer *sine die.*

3.

Truth "Homologated"[1]

...This does not mean that we should try to reveal the "whole truth" of Lacan's strategy. That would be rather naive; and even if it were feasible, it would, to say the least, require such detours through the whole of the *Ecrits* (and elsewhere) that it would exceed the limits set for this work.

But this much said (or said again), it happens that while following the web of this text as closely as possible our reading has brought us back on two occasions to the name of Heidegger. Moreover, we are not *forcing* the point here, since (except for the enigmatic sub-inscription which stands in for its place of origin and which seals/conceals, in the somewhat ostentatious evidence of its secret, the unnameable within meaning)[2] the text indeed ends on a page entirely governed by Heideggerian thematics. A page, then, entirely governed by the question of *truth*—of the being of truth and of the truth of being.

It is now time to question Heidegger's *position* more closely. For indeed, it is first a *positing*: a pure evocation or, if one prefers, a pure "call," but apparently not an attempt to use or to read him. After having barely mentioned the Heideggerian philosopheme of "man in the midst of beings" (*E.*, 527/175),[3] Lacan dismisses any doctrinal reference to what he pejoratively calls a "Heideggerianism," not, contrary to his claims, because of a "reflection" which should (or could) immediately be undertaken, but simply in order to posit the name of Heidegger, that is Heidegger himself, as the one we must "speak" about, because he is the one who speaks in an exemplary way:

> When I speak of Heidegger, or rather when I translate
> him, I at least make the effort to leave the speech he
> proffers us its sovereign *signifiance*. (*E.,* 528/175)

It is true that this declaration simply refers to Lacan's translation of Heidegger's "Logos" in the first volume of *La Psychanalyse* (1956).[4] Moreover (and in that context), that translation and publication are not in themselves insignificant or
negligible. But it is above all not insignificant that it is precisely
this signifiance (that the text will have attempted to manifest all
along) which, once its "sovereignty" has been freed, is said to
belong to Heideggerian "speech." An odd displacement of this
theme onto a master text. One might say it is a way of not *reading* that speech, avoiding or refusing to read it (but then again is
it possible to *read speech*?).[5] One might also say that there is a
certain irresponsibility (or too much cleverness) in jumping
like this, in a flash, from one level to the other, and in "miracu-
lously" solving the whole difficulty of *signifiance* in an invocation, however pure it may be. But if there is indeed something
like a movement of this kind here, or if we are faced, in any
case, with a solution or a completion (where the entirety of
what is deferred in the text would stop and come to rest), nothing prevents it from also being the necessary repetition of that
mise-en-abyme (and probably the last as if paradoxically one
could reach its bottom) which governs Lacan's whole text, both
in its structure and most salient effects. In that case, Lacan's
text could very well appear, in the final analysis, as the machination of a long metonymical chain of which Heidegger would
be the last *name,* and *logos* the last *word,* or if one prefers, the
master-word.

This is why, moreover, one should not neglect to refer here
to the text "Logos" and to its translation, that is, in fact—however implicitly or allusively—to the *concepts* of *logos* and translation. Perhaps *signifiance* itself is no stranger to either of them; it
is perhaps, more precisely, only conceivable on the basis of the
enigmatic relation that Logos, as such, has always maintained

with the notion of translation. We would be too hasty to claim, without being more careful, that the question of *logos* (or the question of being and meaning—or of being as meaning) will always have been comprehended in a general economy of exchange, equivalence, and adequation—in a kind of system (one not as simple as it seems) of the translatable and the untranslatable, of transparency and obstacle. For the moment at least, we can recall that it is precisely this question of translation which runs through the entirety of Heidegger's text, and as one of the fundamental questions of its very constitution. This cannot, in turn, fail to implicate Lacan's translation of "Logos"— especially since "Logos," as one might suspect, is one of those texts which are entirely concerned with a (the) problem of (the) translation. But, we know that it is precisely this problem (in its very ambivalence) that compels Heidegger on the one hand to pulverize the translation of the word itself (moreover under the authority of Heraclitus' word, which, from the beginning, was indeed meant to be translated) and, on the other hand, to neutralize this pulverisation or shattering, by leaving the word simply untranslated. Consequently, when Lacan "leaves Heidegger's speech" its "sovereign *signifiance*," he also preserves this suspension of translation; and when translating, he translates the untranslatable. Or, at the end of the itinerary, we should at least assume that the translation definitively (absolutely?) establishes Logos, taken from the Heideggerian text, as untranslatable. It is moreover in order to respect this second ambivalence that we will speak from now on of the (non)translation of Heidegger.

But translating is also the work one has to carry out with respect to Freud. It begins by rendering *Traumdeutung,* we recall, by "signifiance du rêve" (*E.,* 510). Here translating, as in the case of Heidegger's text, means translating from German. But we know that the whole difficulty of what we have called the (in)articulation of the text resides, in fact, in the apparent (or relative) innocence of this gesture. This difficulty amounts to having to translate all of Freudian conceptuality (which has been taken into account) into linguistic conceptuality (itself already well-worked by Freud). Now, in its very circularity, this practice of translation in fact reproduces, *mutatis mutandis,* the Heideggerian practice of translation—for instance, if we must insist on this, the "translation of Greek into Greek" at work in "Logos" (and elsewhere⁶) which precedes, founds, and—as we have just seen—renders the translation of Greek into German nearly impossible. Moreover, it is not forcing matters to recognize the play of the Heideggerian model itself in the violence Lacan imposes on the Freudian text and in the apparent arbitrariness or license with which he treats it. In reality, what is at stake here is a whole practice of reading governed by the motif of the *unthought.* Just as Heidegger attempts to decipher the unthought of philosophy, Lacan endeavours to locate, in Saussure and Freud (and in a few others as well), the common unthought which founds the possibility of their relation. And this is presumably all the more so—here too the specular paradigm is at work—since, from the unthought to the unconscious (or from the unconscious to the unthought?) there is, as it were, only one step.⁷

The quite simple result is that we must further complicate the apparatus of (in)articulation. We must introduce a third "character" between Freud and Saussure—more precisely perhaps, a *Deus ex machina*—in such a way that the reciprocal translatability of Freud and Saussure ultimately rests on that (non)translation of Heidegger we just mentioned.

One can recognize in Heidegger's *position* the ultimate repetition of the (in)articulation, namely the last effect of the *burning.*⁸ And it is from the *hole* burned in the text that, finally, what we will henceforth understand as "sovereign *significance*" "utters" itself. A voice from *beyond the text* [*outre-texte*] which *is not* quite, however, "the voice of no one," and if it is not that of the *deus ex machina* itself, it is at least that of the prompter.... More seriously, all this amounts to saying that what we thought we could consider under the concept of *diversion* is thus ruled from afar and from above by Heidegger himself. Or to be more precise, the operation mounted against

Heidegger both regulates and diverts diversion itself, since ultimately it reduces the whole difficulty of translatability, and, as it is resolved in the pure nomination of the Heideggerian gesture, it thus refers to a sort of primary language which guarantees all exchanges—to the self-transparency or absolute presence of Logos, itself designated by Heidegger. Diversion is thus nullified in its principle: the resolution of translation abolishes the possibility of assessing any infidelity. Only the principle of pure fidelity, in transparency and in-difference, prevails.

But indifference here does not designate anything like an "anarchic" practice of the text. On the contrary, the issue is rather to preserve rigorously, in this invocation of *logos* (and, we will see, of truth), the possibility beyond the text (and thus also beyond the system) of a sort of "medium" of equivalence where all question of translation of Saussure into Freud, of Freud into Hegel (or into Rousseau or Descartes), of each of the names (or rather of each the texts) into all the others, is erased. From now on, the beyond-the-text [*l'outre-texte*], which is to say *signifiance,* allows for all operations in the "text" itself. The entire movement of strategy will thus have succeeded, because it nullifies its diversion of symbolic logic by reproducing the ideal of *logic*—that is, the transparent language of a universal and exhaustive exchange. This is why everything functions, and functions perfectly.

But this is not all. Freud also appears beyond the text, or, more properly, covers on this last page an operation which is itself without *reading,* per se—which remains in the order or register of simple designation. Immediately after having appealed to Heidegger, Lacan similarly states—but this time in order to exceed all relation to the Freudian text—

> If I speak of being and the letter, if I distinguish the
> other and the Other, it is because Freud shows me that
> they are the terms to which must be referred the
> effects of resistance and transference against which, in
> the twenty years I have engaged in what we will call

after him the impossible practice of psychoanalysis, I
have done unequal battle. (*E.,* 528/175)

The beyond-the-text, then, is (psychoanalytic) *experience*
or *practice.* But what relation do they maintain with Logos, or
with truth? Why are they introduced here? Should we con-
clude from this that Heidegger does not play what we believed
to be his role? Or does this return *of* Freud (if it complicates,
completes, or even explicates this apparatus) ultimately leave
Heidegger's *position* unchanged?

We have been able to note (at least twice) that psychoanalytic experience has been invoked in quite precise strategic
places (when its motif has not been used to evoke a rather
imprecise model of experimental scientificity), and invoked in
order to break, authoritatively, the resistance of a text. At first
it was a question of circumventing the difficult question of the
simultaneous division of the two "kingdoms" of the signifier
and the signified that Saussure postulated at the basis of the
functioning of language, in order to introduce the theory of
anchoring points (*E.,* 503/154).[9] Second, it was a question of
"subverting" the assurance of self-identity assumed, until now,
by the Cartesian *cogito;* it was then the empiricity of desire itself
which came to shatter this "truth" [*évidence*] (*E.,* 517/166).[10]
The eruption of experience (*and experience here is, always,*
desire) has thus taken place each time at the same point or in
the same moment in the text of linguistics as well as in the text
of philosophy, when the issue was to ensure the crossing of the
bar, that is, when the issue was to produce *significance* itself in
order to cross the bar while maintaining it.

But if this is really the case, it can only mean one thing: as in
the case of *logos* (truth), experience (desire) is itself perfectly
(un)translatable, that is, immediately equivalent to its pure
utterance or pure enunciation. Thus, (Freudian) desire occupies the same *position* as (Heideggerian) truth: the beyond-the-
text is the locus (the non-locus, rather) where desire and truth
are gathered and arranged together. This is a twofold (un)trans-

latable which nevertheless *articulates* Lacan's discourse insofar as the true voice of desire (or the desiring voice of truth) is "articulated," and "speaks" in this discourse.

But we see that this "apparatus" can only function on the condition of not only presupposing the problematic of truth in the invocation of *logos* and the question of desire in the appeal to experience (which is relatively easy), but also (and above all) of identifying truth with desire and hearing them *speak* together as *signifiance* itself (without their signal being jammed). Its final liberation closes the text and retrospectively decides both its structure and general economy. But before being able to claim, in such a peremptory (or summary) way, that desire *is* truth (to what extent, in fact, can one deduce essence from position, concept from structure?), perhaps it would be beneficial to listen to that voice of desire a little more. For it happens, precisely, that this voice does not speak. It does not really articulate. It cries out. Surely this could still be heard (if not, properly speaking, listened to). Now it also happens that this cry cannot be heard, for it is the unutterable cry of the symptom (*E.,* 519/168).[11] The voice of desire is thus voiceless. Desire does not speak, it manifests itself. Then on what basis can one speak of the cry of the symptom? How can the visible and the audible be joined, and "speech and phenomena" coincide, *symptôme oblige*?[12]

The answer is well known: the symptom is a metaphor: "metaphor in which flesh or function is taken as a signifying element" (*E.,* 518/166). But this answer in fact leads us backward— prior to the ultimate moment when *signifiance* itself is freed— unless we add, as is done in the last lines of the text, that "if the symptom is a metaphor it is not a metaphor to say so, any more than to say that man's desire is a metonymy" (*E.,* 528/175). Or even more so if we add that "the symptom *is* a metaphor whether one likes it or not, as desire *is* a metonymy, however funny people may find the idea" (*E.,* 528/175). For in this italicized verb from which all metaphorical power is removed in one blow (in spite of the privilege, although necessary, which is granted here to metaphor over metonymy), one can see the appearance "in a lightning moment" (*E.,* 520/168) of being itself in its pure and literal *signifiance*—that is, in its *truth.* Lacan, moreover, does not fail to underscore this immediately:

> Finally if I am to rouse you to indignation over the fact that, after so many years of religious hypocrisy and philosophical bravado, nothing yet has been validly articulated as to *what links metaphor to the question of being and metonymy to its lack...* (*E.,* 528/175, our emphasis)

A remarkable expression in its very imbalance, for if metonymy as such is linked to the lack of being, then the question of being to which *metaphor* is linked is nothing other than the *presence* of being—even if it is thought, as we will see, in its fundamental duplicity (a non-simple presence which includes lack, just as metaphor dominates, founds and precedes metonymy).

Consequently, to the extent that desire is thought according to the (non-simple) opposition of metaphor and metonymy, it is in fact comprehended in a general ontology, and in the last analysis considered according to the classical oppositions: presence/absence, manifestation/withdrawal, etc. Certainly, desire is not to be considered *as* truth. Desire *is* truth (in the same way that symptom *is* metaphor). Nonetheless, this amounts to saying that in the last *instance,* one must refer desire to truth.

This is why, in fact, Freud does not occupy quite the same *position* as Heidegger in this final apparatus. If, as we have seen, the principle which ultimately rules this apparatus (and consequently the whole text) is that of the *mise-en-abyme,* it is not surprising then—but is particularly revealing—that on this same page, Freud's "intangible but radical revolution" is presented as "the symptom...of a putting into question of man in the midst of beings" (*E.,* 527175). For if "man in the midst of beings" is a Heideggerian philosopheme (as is the critical reference in the very last lines to "humanistic man"), it amounts to saying quite simply: Freud is the symptom of Heidegger.

Presumably, this is not so much because Freud designates (or would allow the designation of) the trace, the echo, or the working of desire in Heidegger, but because Heideggerian truth in fact allows the "deciphering" (the translating) of the symptom as "language" or true voice of desire, however speechless, in Freud. Since there is ultimately no metaphorical functioning of metaphor (remaining faithful to Heidegger),[13] to say that Freud is the symptom (the metaphor) of Heidegger is finally to recognize that Heidegger himself is *literally* the truth of Freud or, if one prefers, the *propriety* of the Freudian *letter.*

Thus the entire movement which we have just followed gathers itself *in extremis,* at the point of a "word" on metaphor —on the impossibility of treating metaphor metaphorically, when dealing with desire (with truth), or, as well, in the *thesis* of the Heideggerean truth. Through this, the text finally "anchors itself."[14]

What remains to be considered here is what this truth is about. Not that we should have to wonder whether or not it is Heidegger's truth (although if Heidegger serves to found the practice of diversion, the question of faithfulness to Heidegger's text is not unimportant), but rather, in order to understand what kind of reading is implicated in all this, what silently sustains this sort of final incantation.

This question could certainly elicit a brutal response. Indeed, if we have been able to show that in the last instance (and the reader will recognize that we do not use this word accidentally) Heidegger dominates Lacan's entire strategy, and if this strategy consists, finally, in a "destruction" of the ontology of the sign itself (after and through a diverted or diverting reconstitution of the entire system of ontology), then it is indeed not only a question of a faithful reading, but also of a reading which goes so far as to accompany, in one of its most decisive advances, the entire enterprise of the Heideggerian "destruction" of metaphysics. This is the case, at least from a certain perspective, insofar as the Heideggerian strategy openly implies, at the outset, the "destruction" of the systematics of the *sign* as such (which cannot be said without precautions, we know, for Heidegger's work on language especially avoids a *frontal* attack on the question of the sign). In any case, one can read, in the entire operation mounted by Lacan against the Saussurean sign, an operation directed against the determination of truth as *homoiosis* or *adequatio*—and intended to undo it. To bar the sign is to bar the adequation of the signifier to the signified, that is to say, as we have seen, to the referent. This was perfectly illustrated by the apologue of the two children, itself presented as "the actual experience of truth" (*E.,* 500/151), for if, in spite of the rails, a truth (the truth, that of the hole) could *present itself,* it did not present itself according to the law of re-presentation, that is, according to the law of intelligibility. Now what else is this truth, in its pure presentation— *as* presentation, or, as a *presence* given in the very movement of withdrawing itself from representation—if not ἀλήθεια itself, the concealment/unconcealment that Heidegger always (or almost always) opposed to what is merely a "later" epochal determination of it (an interpretation for which Plato is essentially responsible)? This is a "homoiotical" interpretation of truth which is precisely founded on a "previous" account of the problems raised by the question of the truth of discourse (that is, by the question of falsehood), and on an approach to *aletheia* based on a concern for the "accuracy of enunciation."[15]

This is at least what one can attribute to Heidegger—and certainly with good reason, since a fair number of texts seem to speak in this vein. Provided, that is, that we do not go into detail or neglect Heidegger's extreme caution and overlook the hesitations or regrets, the more or less explicit disavowals which punctuate his *text.*

For what this text ultimately suggests, and even (if however the augmentative is suitable here) makes clear, is that aletheia on the one hand can probably never be reduced to the simple unity of clearing and withdrawing, or of concealment and unconcealment, etc.,[16] and on the other hand, that neither can it be associated with homoiosis as a result of a specific historical "accident." It is, on the contrary, because "as such" (if this can still mean something here), truth (aletheia) will "always" have been caught in the homoiotical interpretation—or at least comprehended in this interpretation—that it has been in fact, until now, the *unthought* of philosophy (including Greek *thought,* which is strictly speaking pre-philosophical, or pre-Platonic) and that on the basis of which the destruction of ontology can be undertaken through the repetition of metaphysics.[17]

This is why, moreover, we could say that in his reading of Freud, Lacan relates the unconscious to the unthought (so defined) just as he refers desire to truth. Yet Lacan does not follow Heidegger as far as this laborious, although systematic, blurring of the aletheia/homoiosis opposition. Quite to the contrary, he reinforces it—for at least in his eyes, the destruction of the sign depends on the rigor of that opposition. In other words, Lacan remains, if you will, within the (most) simple determination of aletheia: the unity of the veiling/unveiling difference—which is to say, as well, in (the most) *dialectical* determination of truth, in the Hegelian sense. Hence, it is not surprising to find that, because it invalidates itself in reduplicating itself, metaphor prevails over metonymy in the final process of literalization (of presentation). Neither is it surprising that we are able to inscribe two "agencies" of truth on the rim of the circle of the system: homoiosis itself, guaranteed by the contract (the Other), and aletheia in the self-presence of the pure adequation of enunciation ("I, the truth, I speak..."), that is to say, in its presence beyond language. It is above all not surprising that we can read such a proposition elsewhere in "Seminar on 'The Purloined Letter'":

> As well, when we are open to hearing the way in which Martin Heidegger discloses to us in the word ἀληθής the play of truth, we rediscover a secret to which truth has always initiated her lovers, and through which they learn that it is in hiding that she offers herself to them *most truly.* (*E.,* 21/*P.,* 37.)

By repeating its own truth within itself, aletheia can be identified as homoiosis. This is quite different than taking (or producing at the extreme edge of thinking) aletheia as "never" having escaped the metaphysical determination of homoiosis. It is consequently homoiosis "itself," or the homoiotical aletheia which will have governed *The Agency of the Letter* through and through. In the apologue of the two children, it is what assigned the brother and the sister to their *proper* places. It is also what, as it instituted the sign as algorithm, also inscribed it in scientific discourse. It is that through which the "truth" of Lacan's discourse—which enunciates or announces the irremediable difference of the subject to itself through the linguistic model of the *shifter*—utters itself (without knowing it?) in/as a perfect adequation of its statement to its enunciation [("I speak..." and Lacan himself: "If I speak of the letter and of being..." (*E.,* 528)]. It is finally what ensures, in spite of everything, the reappropriation of meaning in metaphor, for if the sheaf is not Booz, the abolition of the name is literally the murder of the father. *The title of the letter* is precisely this truth.

We perhaps see now that such a reappropriation could, paradoxically, only be disrupted by the very thing which had to be inscribed in reserve outside of the system: namely by ἀλήθεια, which, ever since Heidegger's text, disturbs, weakens or cracks the entire discourse of metaphysics.

But then *truth* is no longer what is in question. Moreover, to say precisely what is in question is presumably impossible. We shall speak therefore, in the end, of *text*—if the text (is what) does not allow itself to be comprehended in the economy of truth. This has nothing to do with that "text" that Lacan led us to qualify as discourse. Rather, it is a text which Lacan's discourse, despite the disruptions of its enunciation, the gaps in its language, the detours of its process fails to rejoin—or rather in which his discourse never loses itself. Certainly, all discourse is always, also, a text. But *as discourse,* it can only "be" this text insofar as it constantly says, with respect to the text it implies: *I do not want to know,* if we may here single out Freud's text in the discourse we are (inevitably) holding, or by which we are (inevitably) held. And isn't this "denial" precisely what brings Lacan's text (discourse) to a close with the very formula of ontology, that is, with the definition of metaphor? And if what is said about metonymy is not a metaphor, then no metonymy could ever reopen this text onto the "lack" of being.

That, nevertheless, the rhetoricity of the rhetorical cannot be denied,[18] that metaphoricity in general must slide—that it can never settle or stop—is indeed what Freud's text indicated. For that reason, we thought it could be placed as an epigraph. A text which, consequently, has to be re-read....

Notes

1. T.N. In French, *homologuer* means: to certify, to ratify, or to sanction. We have chosen to render *La vérité "homologuée"* as "Truth 'Homologated.'" The English term "homologate" has a semantic range which includes: to ratify, or to represent as agreeing with something else. "Homologated" retains the play in *homologuée* on homoiosis and logos.

2. "T.t.v.m.u.p.t. 14–26 May 1957," *E.,* 528. This chain of punctuated letters approximates most closely the procedure by which Lacan already "lightened" the epigraph of *Function and Field of Speech* in order to "lay bare the purity of its message" in a barbarous parody of language, *E.,* 237/30, 299/110–11. Here and there, one must perhaps understand that the text "written in an unknown language" is "ready," as in the apologue of the two children, "to be charged with signification" (*E.,* 504/155).

3. T.N. Translation slightly modified.

4. T.N. See Martin Heidegger, "Logos" (Heraclitus, Fragment B 50) in *Early Greek Thinking: The Dawn of Western Philosophy,* trans., David Farrell Krell and Frank A. Capuzzi (San Francisco: Harper & Row, 1984).

5. This would be the case if Heidegger was not *read* in *The Agency* or did not govern, if you will, its writing through a certain

reference to this same text "Logos." Did not the signifying decomposition of the tree (*E.,* 504/155), where we have already *heard,* as it were, signifiance cross the bar, end with a call to "the slow maturation of being into the Eν Πάντα of language" (an expression where one can indeed recognize an echo of the Heideggerian treatment and translation of Heraclitus)? Perhaps Heidegger was, thus, if one may risk this expression, already hidden in the tree....

6. A long "theoretical" justification of this (or a long "meditation") can also be found in the part of the course *What is Called Thinking?* devoted to Parmenides. Thus, for instance, in the following text: "The question of That which calls on us to think gives us the mandate to translate the words Ἐὸν Ἔμμεναι. But have they not been translated into the Latin *ens* and *esse,* into our "being" and "to be"? It is indeed superfluous to translate Ἐὸν Ἔμμεναι into Latin or our language. But it is indeed necessary for us to translate these words finally into Greek. Such translation is possible only through a transposition into what speaks from these words. And this translation can succeed only by a leap, the leap of a single vision which sees what the words Ἐὸν Ἔμμεναι, heard with Greek ears, state or tell." Translated by J. Glenn Gray (Harper & Row, 1968), p. 232, slightly modified.

7. To prevent the analogy from being "overwhelming," one would still have to clearly mark the differences: For instance, Heidegger's unswerving refusal to read Freud (to our knowledge), or even to consider the emergence and existence of psychoanalysis; on the other hand, Lacan's emphasis on the epistemological and scientific motifs to the detriment of ontology (at least explicitly, or rather, officially). But these differences are too obvious and too well known for us to insist on them any further.

8. Cf. *TL.,* p. 83.

9. Cf. Ibid., p. 54–55.

10. Cf. Ibid., p. 98.

11. "It is the truth of what this desire has been in his history that the patient cries out through his symptom, as Christ said that the stones themselves would have cried out if the children of Israel had not lent them their voice," *E.,* 518/167.

12. This coincidence would indeed paradoxically make the *aphonia* of desire coincide with the ideality of the pure *voice, phoné*

with *phoneme,* as Derrida was able to exhibit in *Speech and Phenomena,* where one can read, for example, the following: "The ideality of the object, which is only its being-for a nonempirical consciousness, can only be expressed in an element whose phenomenality does not have worldly form. *The name of this element is the voice. The voice is heard.* Phonic signs ("acoustical images" in Saussure's sense, or the phenomenological voice) are "heard" by the subject who proffers them in the absolute proximity of their present. The subject does not have to pass forth beyond himself to be immediately affected by his expressive activity," *Speech and Phenomena,* trans., David Allison (Evanston: Northwestern University Press, 1973), p. 76. But this paradox is presumably ready to be solved, as in the case of any paradox, if one thinks of the decisive, or even crucial, importance that *speech* takes on in the entire Lacanian apparatus—that *speech* is where, as we saw, the privilege of a certain linguistic model, the necessary mode of exposition for Lacan's "training" discourse, and finally the *truth* introduced by this discourse (the truth which "speaks") are established.

13. Or, more precisely, and in order to make this indication more explicit in as brief a space as possible: There is no metaphorical functioning of metaphor if one retains above all (this time being faithful to what Lacan allows us to understand in his way of evoking Heidegger) everything in the texts of Heidegger that puts his enterprise of re-reading Greek (through"etymology," "translation," etc.), the "original" philosophical language, under the authority of a fundamental *literality* that one must understand anew, rather than under that of a metaphoricity that one would have to decipher. Among so many others, the text "Logos" would bear witness to this.

14. This anchoring of discourse hence forms a system [through the priviledge granted to metaphor (in sum, against difference)] with Lacan's preference for the paradigmatic (vertical) axis of language over syntagmatic linearity—and consequently, with the fundamental reference to poetry, or a no less fundamental recourse to a poetic *style,* cf. *TL.,* 56–57 and 73–74. Poetry is that desire or that will of an *anchored* language. Hence, the eventual diversion of diversion (that is to say its re-turn and cancellation), which corresponds, as we will see, to the movement of reappropriation here begun and founded—and thanks to which the *connotative sliding,* which constitutes diversion, falls back on a pure denotation. We will note that a similar privilege is granted to poetry by Heidegger, with the difference however

that Heidegger deliberately refuses even to use the philosopheme *metaphor,* and it is here undoubtedly that the "question" of the Heideggerian *text* should be taken into account (cf. for example, *Der Satz vom Grund,* forthcoming as *The Principle of Reason,* trans., Reginald Lilly (Bloomington: Indiana University Press, 1991): "The metaphorical exists only within the boundaries of metaphysics." For all this we refer the reader to Derrida's "White Mythology," in *Margins of Philosophy,* trans., Alan Bass (Chicago University Press, 1982).

15. This is a well-known thesis found in the Heideggerian reading of the allegory of the cave, "La doctrine de Platon sur la vérité," in *Questions II* (Gallimard, 1968). Originally published as: *Platons Lehre von der Wahreit,* from lectures of 1930–31 and 1933–34.

16. This is not the place to demonstrate it. But we can indicate, at least, that by reading the most "daring" texts of Heidegger closely, it always seems that, between the clearing and the withdrawing, in (between) their unity, a supplementary *trait* inserts itself, which is known (to refer to a text in the third part of the "Origin of the Work of Art") as the *attraction* (*Zug*) of truth towards the work which is "in the essence of truth." *Poetry, Language, Thought,* trans., Albert Hofstadter (New York: Harper & Row, 1971), p. 46.

17. We refer, among others, to the "corrections" made in the text on Plato cited earlier, in the conference entitled "The End of Philosophy and the Task of Thinking" trans., Joan Stambaugh, in *Basic Writings* (New York: Harper & Row, 1977).

18. A denial, moreover, which often comes back in Lacan: cf., for example, *E.,* 260/51, "Radiophonie" *Scilicet* 2/3, p.72.

Index